CHOPSTICKS RECIPES

TRADITIONAL DISHES

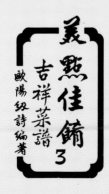

美點佳餚
吉祥菜譜
歐陽敏詩編著
3

Published and Distributed by

Chopsticks Publications Ltd.

P.O. Box 73515, Kowloon Central Post Office, Kowloon, Hong Kong.
108 Boundary St., G/F, Kowloon, Hong Kong.
Tel.: 336 8433   339 0454
Fax: (852) 336 8287

ISBN 962 7018 63 5
Photography by Au-yeung Chiu Mei
Edited by Caroline Au-yeung

UK Sole Distributor:
Gazelle Book Services Ltd
Falcon House Queen Square
Lancaster LA1 1RN
England

出版者及總批發
嘉饌出版有限公司

香港　九龍中央郵箱73515號
香港　九龍界限街108號地下
電話：336 8433, 339 0454
傳眞：（852）336 8287

FOREWORD

Traditional Dishes is the third cookbook in the Chopsticks Recipes series. As the title suggests, this cookbook contains basically traditional recipes passed on from generation to generation for centuries, with improvement and changes made to suit the habits and appetite of most people nowadays. Most dishes included in this book are cooked during Chinese New Year or other important festivals and special occasions such as weddings and child births.

Chinese New Year, which falls around mid-January to mid-February according to the Julian calendar, is the most important time of the year for the Chinese people. Not only does the festival symbolize a fresh start to a new year full of resolutions, it is also a celebration of togetherness and unity for the whole family. During this time, all members of the family, usually consisting of a few generations, gather together to celebrate for as long as twenty days. Many delicious meals are prepared for friends and relatives. Due to the superstition of our ancestors, the dishes are named after different signs of good luck; these names are still used today for the spirit of the old-fashioned celebrations.

In the contents, we have put down the name of each dish and what it is made up of. Every dish is a symbol of something good — may all the goodness come to those who try these dishes.

Cecilia J. Au-yang

CONTENTS

目錄

富貴有餘
Abalone in Oyster Sauce

材料：

鮑魚1磅（ ½ 公斤 ）
粗鹽2湯匙
生粉1湯匙
水6杯
酒1茶匙
羌3片
葱3棵

油5湯匙
豬皮2片
上湯1杯
生菜1磅（ ½ 公斤 ）
葱頭1粒
蒜頭1粒

調味－酒 1 茶匙
　　　蠔油 2 湯匙
　　　糖 2 茶匙
　　　胡椒粉少許

饋料－生粉 1 茶匙
　　　水 1 湯匙
　　　老抽 ¼ 茶匙

製法：

* 鮑魚用粗鹽及生粉擦淨，置水喉下沖洗透澈，盛起候用。
* 鑊中放入 2 杯清水煮沸，倒入鮑魚飛水 ½ 分鐘。
* 鍋燒紅，潑酒加入水 2 杯，羗片及葱。將鮑魚放入以文火煮 1 小時。停火離凍後。再煮30分鐘。重複 2 次後即將羗葱棄去。
* 瓦鍋燒熱加油 1 湯匙，將一片豬皮放在鍋底，鮑魚排放在上倒入上湯，另用一塊豬皮蓋住鮑魚。以中火煮沸後，轉用文火焗20分鐘。棄去豬皮，取出鮑魚切片。鮑魚汁留起候用。
* 生菜洗淨放入餘下 2 杯沸水中加油 2 湯匙飛水，隔去水份排放在長碟上。葱蒜頭切片。
* 鑊燒熱加入餘油煮沸，爆香葱、蒜片。倒入鮑魚片炒透。潑酒加鮑魚汁及調味料。試妥味後以生粉水埋饋，隨即淋在生菜上即成。

Ingredients:

1 lb (½ kg) abalone
2 tbsp coarse salt
1 tbsp cornflour
6 cups water
1 tsp wine
3 slices ginger
3 spring onions
5 tbsp corn oil
2 pieces pork skin
1 cup stock
1 lb (½ kg) lettuce
1 shallot
1 garlic clove

Seasoning-
1 tsp wine
2 tbsp oyster sauce
2 tsp sugar
a pinch of pepper

Gravy Mix-
1 tsp cornflour
1 tbsp water
¼ tsp dark soy

Method:

* Rub and clean the abalone with the coarse salt and the cornflour. Rinse thoroughly.
* Bring 2 cups of the water to boil in a wok and blanch the abalone for half a minute then drain.
* Heat a saucepan; sprinkle the wine and put in another 2 cups of water, the ginger and the spring onions. Place in the abalone to simmer for 1 hour over low heat. Leave to cool then reboil for 30 minutes. Repeat twice then discard the ginger and spring onions.
* Heat a casserole with 1 tbsp of the oil and place a piece of the pork skin into it. Arrange the abalone on top then pour in the stock. Cover the abalone with the other piece of the pork skin. Bring to the boil over moderate heat then leave to simmer for 20 minutes. Discard the pork skin. Remove and slice the abalone. Retain the sauce for later use.
* Wash the lettuce and blanch in the remaining 2 cups of water with 2 tbsp of the oil. Drain and arrange on to the platter. Slice the shallot and garlic.
* Bring the remaining oil to boil in a heated wok and sauté the shallot and garlic. Pour in the abalone to stir fry thoroughly. Sizzle the wine then pour in the abalone sauce and the seasoning. Thicken the sauce with the gravy mix. Scoop on to the lettuce and serve hot.

前程錦繡
Assorted Meat Combination

鹵水料：

陳皮1方吋
溫水¼杯
八角1湯匙
小茴1茶匙
甘草1茶匙
桂皮1方吋
羌3片
水6杯

調味料－鹽¼茶匙
　　　　糖4安（112克）
　　　　酒3湯匙
　　　　生抽2杯

材料：

豬脷1條
牛腸1磅（½公斤）
沸水5杯
蔴油2湯匙
熟冬菇6隻
火腿½磅（224克）
罐頭鮑魚1罐
海蜇½磅（224克）
凍水3杯

生抽 1 湯匙
白切雞½隻
番茄 2 個
綠車厘子數粒

製法：

* 陳皮以溫水浸至軟。將鹵水料洗淨
與薑片及陳皮一同放入紗布袋內紮
緊。深鍋一個加水，將紮妥之鹵水
料投入鍋內以中火煮沸後，將火轉
慢續煮 1 小時。加入調味料煮片刻
試妥味。
* 豬胴及牛腒浸於 4 杯沸水中 3 分鐘
，取出豬胴刮去胴苔與牛腒置水喉
下沖洗乾淨。一同放入鹵水中慢火
焓 1 小時。取出攤凍以蔴油 1 湯匙
塗面切薄片候用。
* 冬菇，火腿及鮑魚皆切片。
* 海蜇放入餘下沸水中略拖，取出過
冷河隔乾水份，轉放入凍水中浸 1
小時，隔去水份後加生抽及餘下蔴
油略醃，排放在碟中央。
* 豬胴，牛腒，冬菇，火腿及鮑魚分
別砌成葉子形，圍着海蜇。
* 白切雞斬件覆蓋在海蜇之上。
* 番茄切片與綠色車厘子伴碟作裝飾
。

Spicy Sauce Ingredients:

1 sq. in. (2.5 cm²) tangerine peel
¼ cup warm water
1 tbsp star anise
1 tsp cumin
1 tsp liquorice
1 sq. in. (2.5 cm²) cinnamon peel
3 slices ginger
6 cups water

Seasoning-
¼ tsp salt
4 oz (112 g) sugar
3 tbsp cooking sherry
2 cups light soy

Ingredients:

1 pig's tongue
1 lb (½ kg) beef shin
5 cups boiling water
2 tbsp sesame oil
6 large cooked Chinese mushrooms
½ lb (224 g) ham
1 tin abalone
½ lb (224 g) jelly fish
3 cups cold water
1 tbsp light soy
½ poached chicken
2 tomatoes
a few green cherries

Method:

* Soak the tangerine peel in the
warm water until softened. Wash
all the dry ingredients and put in a
muslin bag with the ginger and
tangerine peel. Place in a saucepan
with the water and bring to the
boil over moderate heat. Lower
the heat to simmer for an hour.
Add the seasoning and boil for a
further minute. Adjust the
flavour.
* Soak the pig's tongue and beef
shin in 4 cups of the boiling water
for 3 minutes and remove. Scrape
off the white skin from the pig's
tongue. Wash both items under a
running tap, then put into the
boiling spicy sauce to simmer for
an hour over low heat. Remove
and leave to cool. Coat with 1 tbsp
of the sesame oil and slice.
* Slice the mushrooms, ham and
abalone.
* Wash the jelly fish, scald in the
remaining boiling water and refresh. Soak in the cold water for 1
hour. Drain and marinate with the
soy sauce and the remaining tbsp
of sesame oil. Place in the centre
of the plate.
* Arrange the sliced pig's tongue,
beef skin, mushrooms, ham and
abalone separately on a plate into
the shape of a leaf around the jelly
fish.
* Chop the poached chicken and
place on to the jelly fish.
* Garnish with the sliced tomatoes
and green cherries. Serve cold.

全家福祿
Assorted Meat in Brown Sauce

材料：

魷魚 1 隻
鷄肉 2 安（56克）
海參 1 隻
沸水 5 杯
羌 4 片
葱 4 棵
瑤柱 1 粒
熟冬菇 4 隻
紅蘿蔔 3 安（84克）

火腿 2 安（56克）
鮑魚 1 隻
油 1 湯匙

醃鷄料—酒 1 茶匙
　　　　羌汁 1 茶匙
　　　　生抽 1 茶匙
　　　　糖 $\frac{1}{2}$ 茶匙
　　　　生粉 1 茶匙

調味－酒 1 湯匙
　　　上湯 3 杯
　　　鹽 ½ 茶匙
　　　生抽 1 茶匙
　　　糖 1 茶匙
　　　胡椒粉少許

饋料－生粉 1 茶匙
　　　水 1 湯匙
　　　老抽 ½ 茶匙
　　　蔴油 1 茶匙

製法：

* 魷魚洗淨切件。
* 雞肉切薄片，放入和勻之醃料中醃
  10分鐘。
* 海參放於 2 杯沸水中加羗片及葱各
  一半飛水約30秒鐘，撈起過冷河隔
  乾水份。
* 瑤柱浸透蒸30分鐘後撕成幼絲。熟
  冬菇切片。
* 紅蘿蔔切片放入另 1 杯沸水中飛水
  。火腿及鮑魚皆切片。餘下一半羗
  葱磨茸候用。
* 將全部生料放入餘下 2 杯沸水中飛
  水，撈起過冷河隔乾水份。
* 燒紅鑊加油煮沸爆香羗、葱茸。灒
  酒加上湯煮沸，倒入全部材料文火
  煮 5 分鐘。調妥味以生粉水埋饋，
  盛在大碗內上桌即可。

Ingredients:

1 squid
2 oz (56 g) chicken meat
1 sea cucumber
5 cups boiling water
4 slices ginger
4 spring onions
1 scallop
4 cooked Chinese mushrooms
3 oz (84 g) bamboo shoots or carrots
2 oz (56 g) ham
1 abalone
1 tbsp corn oil

Chicken Marinade-
1 tsp wine
1 tsp ginger juice
1 tsp light soy
½ tsp sugar
1 tsp cornflour

Seasoning-
1 tbsp wine
3 cups stock
½ tsp salt
1 tsp light soy
1 tsp sugar
a pinch of pepper

Gravy Mix-
1 tsp cornflour
1 tbsp water
½ tsp dark soy
1 tsp sesame oil

Method:

* *Wash and cut the squid into pieces.*
* *Slice the chicken and immerse in the mixed marinade to stir well. Leave aside for 10 minutes.*
* *Blanch the sea cucumber in 2 cups of the boiling water with half of the ginger and spring onions for 30 seconds. Refresh and drain.*
* *Steam and shred the scallop after being soaked for 30 minutes. Slice the mushrooms.*
* *Slice and blanch the bamboo shoots in another cup of the boiling water. Slice the ham and the abalone. Mince the remaining ginger and spring onions for later use.*
* *Blanch all the raw ingredients in the remaining 2 cups of boiling water then refresh and drain.*
* *Heat the wok with the oil to sauté the remaining ginger and spring onions till aromatic. Sizzle the wine and add the stock to bring to boil. Stir in all the ingredients to simmer for 5 minutes. Season to taste and stir in the gravy mix to thicken. Serve hot.*

鴛鴦並蒂
Black and White Mushrooms
in Oyster Sauce

材料：

花菇2安（56克）
沸水4½杯
白菌8安（224克）
生菜1棵
鹽1茶匙
糖1茶匙
油4湯匙
蒜頭1粒切片
葱頭2粒切片
蝦子1湯匙

醃冬菇料－鹽⅛茶匙
　　　　　糖½茶匙
　　　　　油1湯匙

調味料－－鹽¼茶匙
　　　　　酒1茶匙
　　　　　冬菇水½杯
　　　　　蠔油2茶匙
　　　　　糖½茶匙

饋料－－－生粉1茶匙
　　　　　水1湯匙
　　　　　蔴油1茶匙

製法：

* 花菇洗淨放於1½杯沸水中浸至軟，取出剪去蒂，搤出之水份留作上湯候用。將醃料和勻加入拌妥，置蒸籠內蒸12分鐘。
* 白菌放入另1杯沸水中飛水½分鐘，取出過冷河隔乾水份。
* 生菜洗淨放於餘下沸水中加鹽，糖及油2湯匙略拖，撈起隔去水份放在碟上。
* 燒紅鑊加入餘油煮沸，灑下鹽爆香蒜、葱片。倒入白菌及花菇兜勻。潻酒加上湯，調味料及蝦子煮數秒鐘，以生粉水埋饋即可上碟。

Ingredients:

2 oz (56 g) dried Chinese mushrooms
4½ cups boiling water
8 oz (224 g) button mushrooms
1 lettuce
1 tsp salt
1 tsp sugar
4 tbsp corn oil
1 sliced garlic
2 sliced shallots
1 tbsp shrimp roe

Mushroom Marinade-
1/8 tsp salt
½ tsp sugar
1 tbsp corn oil

Seasoning-
¼ tsp salt
1 tsp wine
½ cup mushroom stock
2 tsp oyster sauce
½ tsp sugar

Gravy Mix-
1 tsp cornflour
1 tbsp water
1 tsp sesame oil

Method:

* *Wash and soak the dried mushrooms in 1½ cups of the boiling water for an hour until softened. Cut off the stalks and squeeze out the water to retain as stock. Mix well with the marinade then steam over high heat for 12 minutes.*
* *Blanch the button mushrooms in 1 cup of the boiling water for half a minute. Refresh and drain.*
* *Wash and blanch the lettuce in the remaining boiling water with the salt, sugar and 2 tbsp of the oil. Drain and dish on to a platter.*
* *Drop the remaining oil in the heated wok and sprinkle in the salt. Sauté the garlic and shallots till aromatic. Stir in the 2 kinds of mushrooms to shallow fry thoroughly. Sizzle the wine, add the stock, seasoning and the shrimp roe to cook for a few seconds. Trickle in the gravy mix to thicken the sauce. Dish and serve hot.*

金錢滿掌
Braised Mushrooms with Ducks' Webs

材料：

鴨掌24隻	葱頭2粒
粗鹽2湯匙	八角3粒
沸水3杯	酒1湯匙
老抽2湯匙	油2湯匙
炸油½鑊	蒜片1茶匙
水2杯	熟冬菇2安（56克）
羌3片	葱2棵切度

調味－酒1茶匙
　　　生抽1茶匙
　　　蠔油1湯匙
　　　糖1茶匙
　　　胡椒粉少許

饋料－生粉1茶匙
　　　水1湯匙
　　　老抽¼茶匙
　　　蔴油1茶匙

製法：

* 鴨掌用粗鹽擦淨洗妥，置沸水中煮5分鐘，取出隔淨水份，抹乾後以老抽塗勻。
* 炸油煮沸，將鴨掌放入猛火炸至起泡。撈起置水喉下沖凍隔乾。
* 壓力保一個，將水注入煮沸，倒入鴨掌、羌片、葱頭及八角。蓋上保蓋以慢火炆20分鐘。加入酒再炆10分鐘，挾起排放碟上。鴨掌汁留起候用。
* 燒紅鑊加油煮沸，爆香蒜片，瓚酒加入以上鴨掌汁1杯。隨將鴨掌及熟冬菇放入鑊中煮10分鐘。再加調味料以生粉水埋饋拌勻上碟，葱度灑面即可上桌。

Ingredients:

24 ducks webs
2 tbsp coarse salt
3 cups boiling water
2 tbsp dark soy
½ wok corn oil for deep frying
2 cups water
3 slices ginger
2 shallots
3 star anises
1 tbsp wine
2 tbsp corn oil
1 tsp sliced garlic
2 oz (56 g) cooked Chinese mushrooms
2 sectioned spring onions

Seasoning-
1 tsp wine
1 tsp light soy
1 tbsp oyster sauce
1 tsp sugar
a pinch of pepper

Gravy Mix-
1 tsp cornflour
1 tbsp water
¼ tsp dark soy
1 tsp sesame oil

Method:

* *Rub the ducks' webs with the coarse salt then rinse well. Simmer in the boiling water for 5 minutes then remove and drain. Dry and coat with the dark soy.*
* *Bring the oil to the boil and deep fry the webs over high heat till brown and crisp. Refresh and drain.*
* *Gently bring the water to the boil in a pressure cooker. Put in the webs and the ginger, shallots and star anises. Cover tightly and simmer over low heat for 20 minutes. Pour in the wine and continue to cook for 10 minutes. Remove on to a platter. Retain the juice for later use.*
* *Heat the wok to bring the oil to the boil. Sauté the garlic till aromatic then sizzle the wine and pour in 1 cup of the juice. Return the webs and mushrooms to the wok and simmer for 10 minutes. Add the seasoning and trickle in the gravy mix to stir well. Dish with the spring onions and serve.*

名利雙收
Carps in Casserole

材料：

鯉魚2條，每條重約10安（280克）
羌4安（112克）
葱4安（112克）
芫茜3棵
油4湯匙

調味－紹酒1湯匙
　　　上湯¾杯
　　　鹽¼茶匙
　　　生抽1湯匙
　　　糖1茶匙
　　　胡椒粉少許

饡料－生粉1茶匙
　　　水1湯匙
　　　老抽¼茶匙

製法：

* 活鯉魚用刀將頭部稍拍，劏肚去內臟以毛巾抹淨。魚鱗刮否隨意。
* 羌去皮切厚片後拍扁。留起2湯匙羌絲作點綴。
* 葱洗淨後用刀一切為二。芫茜洗淨摘妥。亦留起2湯匙葱絲作裝飾。
* 瓦鍋燒紅加入油3湯匙將羌、葱爆香。放入鯉魚煎至兩面金黃色。隨即潲酒，倒入上湯，蓋上鍋蓋以中火炆10分鐘。
* 揭起蓋子加入調味品試至合味。若汁料太稀可以生粉水打饡，最後加入餘油1湯匙，灑下羌葱絲及芫茜，原鍋上桌。

Ingredients:

2 live carps, about 10 oz (280 g) each
4 oz (112 g) ginger
4 oz (112 g) spring onions
3 parsley sprigs
4 tbsp corn oil

Seasoning-
1 tbsp yellow wine
¾ cup stock
¼ tsp salt
1 tbsp light soy
1 tsp sugar
a pinch of pepper

Gravy Mix-
1 tsp cornflour
1 tbsp water
¼ tsp dark soy

Method:

* Pat the fish head with the side of the cleaver. Gut, wash and dry with the towel.
* Scrape, slice and pat the ginger. Shred and retain 2 tbsp for garnishing.
* Wash and cut the spring onions into halves. Wash and trim the parsleys. Keep 2 tbsp of the shredded spring onions for garnishing.
* Heat the casserole with 3 tbsp of the oil to sauté the ginger and spring onions. Add the fish to fry until both sides are golden brown. Sizzle the wine and pour in the stock. Cover to simmer over moderate heat for 10 minutes.
* Remove the lid and add the seasoning. Adjust the flavour to taste. If the sauce is runny, stir in the gravy mix to thicken it. Add the remaining tbsp oil to brighten the dish. Scatter the shredded ginger, spring onions and parsley on to the fish and serve hot.

富贵吉祥

Chicken in Pastry

材料：

上鷄1隻約3磅（1½公斤）
粗鹽2湯匙
羌2安（56克）
葱3棵
五香粉2茶匙
鷄粉¼茶匙
榨菜¼磅（112克）
水2杯
豬肉6安（168克）
油2湯匙
網油或蓮葉1塊
批皮4磅（2公斤）

調味料－酒1½湯匙
　　　　鹽1茶匙
　　　　生抽1茶匙
　　　　糖2湯匙

製法：

* 上鷄用粗鹽擦淨後清洗妥當抹乾水
  份。羌切片，葱切度。將五香粉、
  鷄粉、一半羌葱及調味料之一半和
  勻，擦在鷄上及鷄肚內醃½小時
  。將羌、葱棄去。
* 榨菜以水浸10分鐘後切絲。豬肉洗
  淨切絲。將餘下羌、葱亦切幼絲。
* 燒紅鑊加油煮沸，爆炒羌、葱、榨
  菜絲及豬肉絲約30秒。潵酒加餘下
  調味料兜勻，盛起放入鷄肚內。
* 網油用溫水洗淨，攤在桌上將鷄整
  隻包住。
* 批皮以木棍輾成½吋（1.25公分）
  厚。再將鷄放入包妥，置已預開300
  度（煤氣2度）焗爐內焗1小時。
* 取出鷄棄去批皮後，斬件上碟即成。

Ingredients:

1 chicken, about 3 lb (1½ kg)
2 tbsp coarse salt
2 oz (56 g) ginger
3 spring onions
2 tsp five spice powder
¼ tsp chicken powder
¼ lb (112 g) preserved Szechuen
　vegetables
2 cups water
6 oz (168 g) pork
2 tbsp corn oil
1 piece pork net or lotus leaf
4 lb (2 kg) pastry

Seasoning-
1½ tbsp wine
1 tsp salt
1 tsp light soy
2 tbsp sugar

Method:

* Rub the chicken with the salt,
  wash and dry thoroughly. Slice the
  ginger. Section the spring onions.
  Mix the five spice powder, chicken
  powder and half of the ginger,
  spring onions and seasoning in a
  bowl then rub both the inside and
  outside of the chicken and marinate for half an hour. Remove the
  ginger and spring onions.
* Soak the preserved vegetables in
  the water for 10 minutes. Wash
  and shred with the pork. Shred the
  remaining ginger and spring
  onions finely.
* Heat the wok to bring the oil to the
  boil. Sauté the ginger, spring
  onions, preserved vegetables and
  the pork for 30 seconds. Sizzle the
  wine and add the seasoning. Remove and stuff these ingredients
  inside the chicken.
* Wash the pork net with warm
  water and place on the table to
  wrap up the chicken.
* Roll out the pastry to ½" (1.25
  cm) thick and wrap up, enclosing
  the chicken entirely. Bake in a
  preheated oven of 300°F (Gas
  Mark 2) for an hour.
* Remove the chicken from the
  oven. Break the pastry and un-
  wrap the chicken. Cut into serving
  pieces and dish.

添丁添財
Chicken in Sweet Wine

材料：

上鷄 1 隻約 3 磅（ 1½ 公斤 ）
豬肝 4 安（ 112克 ）
上肉 4 安（ 112克 ）
花生 1 杯
木耳 1 安（ 28克 ）
沸水 3 杯
羌 ½ 磅（ 224克 ）
葱頭 1 粒
油 2 湯匙

醃鷄料—羌汁 ¼ 杯　　醃肝料—羌汁 1 茶匙
　　　　酒 ¼ 杯　　　　　　　酒 1 茶匙
　　　　生粉 1 湯匙　　　　　生粉 1 茶匙

醃肉料—生抽 1 茶匙　調味料—糯米酒 3 杯
　　　　糖 ½ 茶匙　　　　　　白酒 2 杯
　　　　酒 ½ 茶匙　　　　　　上湯 4 杯
　　　　生粉 ½ 茶匙　　　　　鹽 1 茶匙
　　　　水 2 湯匙　　　　　　糖 1 茶匙

製法：

* 鷄洗淨切大件，放入醃鷄料中醃30
  分鐘。
* 豬肝切大片，放入醃肝料中醃30分
  鐘候用。
* 上肉切片，加入醃肉料內醃20分鐘。
* 花生洗淨浸 ½ 小時。木耳浸透修剪
  妥當後放於2杯沸水中飛水片刻，
  撈起冲凍隔乾水份。
* 羌去皮洗淨剁成粗粒。葱頭拍扁。
* 燒紅鑊加油煮沸，爆香葱頭棄去，
  再加羌粒爆透，隨即放入鷄件及花
  生兜炒5分鐘。倒下兩種酒再煮沸
  ，轉倒於另一深鍋內加木耳續煮30
  分鐘。
* 豬肝及肉片一同放入餘下沸水中飛
  水撈起後冲凍，加入鷄中再煮5
  分鐘。試妥味後即可離火，取出熱
  食。

Ingredients:

1 chicken, about 3 lb (1½ kg)
4 oz (112 g) pork liver
4 oz (112 g) lean pork
1 cup peanuts
1 oz (28 g) hard black fungus
3 cups boiling water
½ lb (224 g) ginger
1 shallot
2 tbsp corn oil

Chicken Marinade-	*Liver Marinade-*
¼ cup ginger juice	*1 tsp ginger juice*
¼ cup wine	*1 tsp wine*
1 tbsp cornflour	*1 tsp cornflour*

Pork Marinade-
1 tsp light soy　*½ tsp cornflour*
½ tsp sugar　*2 tbsp water*
½ tsp wine

Seasoning-
3 cups glutinous rice wine
2 cups white wine　*1 tsp salt*
4 cups broth　*1 tsp sugar*

Method:

* *Clean and chop the chicken into bite-sized pieces. Soak in the mixed chicken marinade for 30 minutes.*
* *Slice and mix the liver with the liver marinade and leave aside for 30 minutes.*
* *Slice the pork and stir in the mixed pork marinade and marinate for 20 minutes.*
* *Wash and soak the peanuts for half an hour. Soak, trim and blanch the black fungus in 2 cups of the boiling water for a minute. Refresh and drain.*
* *Scrape, wash and dice the ginger coarsely. Mash the shallot.*
* *Heat the wok and bring the oil to boil. Sauté the shallot till fragrant then discard. Add the ginger to sauté well and stir in the chicken and nuts to fry for 5 minutes. Pour in both of the wines to bring to the boil. Transfer into a saucepan and simmer with the fungus for 30 minutes.*
* *Blanch the liver and pork in the remaining cups of boiling water then refresh. Add into the chicken wine and continue to cook for a further 5 minutes. Season to taste. Remove and serve.*

四海昇平
Double-boiled Pigeons with White Fungus

材料：

乳鴿2隻共重1磅（ $\frac{1}{2}$ 公斤 ）
沸水8杯
羗汁2湯匙
葱頭2粒
酒2湯匙
瘦肉4安（112克 ）
雪耳1安（28克 ）
凍水3杯
陳皮 $\frac{1}{2}$ 方吋
羗2片

調味料一酒1茶匙
　　　　鹽 $1\frac{1}{2}$ 茶匙
　　　　糖 $\frac{1}{2}$ 茶匙
　　　　胡椒粉少許

製法：

* 乳鴿洗淨放於4杯沸水中加羗汁、葱頭及酒飛水，取出過冷河隔乾水份。瘦肉亦放同一沸水中飛水，取出置水喉下沖凍。沸水留起候用。
* 雪耳放入凍水中浸2小時至軟，取出剪去蒂後洗淨。放於以上沸水中飛水1分鐘，撈起沖凍隔去水份。
* 陳皮洗淨放於 $\frac{1}{2}$ 杯沸水中浸透。
* 燉盅內放入餘下沸水 $3\frac{1}{2}$ 杯，將乳鴿、瘦肉、陳皮及羗片全部放入。蓋上盅蓋用紗紙貼緊邊沿。
* 另用深鍋一個，放水半鍋，將一條毛巾放在鍋底。隨把燉盅放在毛巾上以文火燉 $1\frac{1}{2}$ 小時。以蒸籠燉亦可。
* 揭開紗布，加入雪耳及調味料。蓋密再燉20分鐘，即可取出熱食。

Ingredients:

2 pigeons, 8 oz (224 g) each
8 cups boiling water
2 tbsp ginger juice
2 shallots
2 tbsp wine
4 oz (112 g) lean pork
1 oz (28 g) white fungus
3 cups cold water
½ sq. in. (2.5 cm²) tangerine peel
2 slices ginger

Seasoning-
1 tsp wine
1½ tsp salt
½ tsp sugar
a pinch of pepper

Method:

* *Wash and blanch the pigeons in 4 cups of the boiling water with the ginger juice, shallots and wine. Remove, refresh and drain. Blanch the pork in the same boiling water then rinse under a running tap. Retain the boiling water for later use.*
* *Soak the white fungus in the cold water for 2 hours until softened. Remove the hard stems and clean. Blanch in the same boiling water for 1 minute. Rinse with the cold water then drain.*
* *Wash and soak the tangerine peel in ½ cup of the boiling water.*
* *Pour the remaining 3½ cups of boiling water into a pot. Add the pigeons, pork, tangerine peel and the ginger then cover with the lid. Seal the slit between the lid and the pot with a strip of paper.*
* *Half fill the saucepan with water. Place a towel at the bottom and put into the pot and simmer for 1½ hours. A steamer can also be used instead of a saucepan.*
* *Remove the paper and add the white fungus and seasoning. Cover to simmer for a further 20 minutes. Remove and serve hot.*

賽雪欺霜
Egg White with Shredded Fish

材料：

魚柳 4 安（112克）	調味料－鹽 ½ 茶匙
蛋白 2 杯（12隻蛋）	胡椒粉少許
油 6 杯	花奶 1 茶匙
另油 2 湯匙起鑊用	濕豆粉 1 湯匙
羌茸 ½ 茶匙	
葱粒 ½ 茶匙	餡料 —— 生粉 1 茶匙
酒 1 茶匙	水 1 湯匙
上湯 ½ 杯	生抽 ½ 茶匙
蛋王 1 隻	糖 ¼ 茶匙
番茄 2 片	
	汁料 —— 芫茜茸 1 茶匙
醃魚料－蛋白 1 茶匙	葱粒 ½ 茶匙
生粉 1 茶匙	生抽 1 茶匙
胡椒粉少許	浙醋 1 茶匙
	蔴油 ½ 茶匙

製法：

* 魚柳洗淨抹乾切幼條，倒入醃魚料中放置一旁醃10分鐘。
* 蛋白打爛放入碗內，加入調味料及魚柳撈勻。
* 燒紅鑊加入油 1 杯煮沸，將鑊搪勻後把油傾回油桶內。再將餘油 5 杯倒入鑊中煮至微溫，蛋白搞勻倒入泡片刻。以鑊鏟略拌至蛋白浮起時，即以罩籬撈起隔去餘油。
* 另鑊燒紅加油 2 湯匙爆香羌、葱茸，瀋酒加上湯再煮沸。即以生粉水打餡，將蛋白重倒入鑊中拌勻上碟。
* 在蛋白中央弄一小洞，加入蛋王 1 隻。將拌勻之芫茜汁淋在上面。最後以番茄片圍邊。即可拌勻進食，味勝螃蟹。

Ingredients:

4 oz (112 g) fish fillet
2 cups egg white (12 eggs)
6 cups corn oil
2 tbsp corn oil for sautéeing
½ tsp minced ginger
½ tsp chopped spring onions
1 tsp wine
½ cup stock
1 egg yolk
2 sliced tomatoes

Fish Marinade-
1 tsp egg white
1 tsp cornflour
a pinch of pepper

Seasoning-
½ tsp salt
a pinch of pepper
1 tsp milk
1 tbsp cornflour mix

Gravy Mix-
1 tsp cornflour
1 tbsp water
½ tsp light soy
¼ tsp sugar

Sauce-
1 tsp chopped parsley
½ tsp chopped spring onions
1 tsp light soy
1 tsp red vinegar
½ tsp sesame oil

Method:

* *Wash, dry and shred the fish. Coat with the marinade then leave aside for 10 minutes.*
* *Whisk the egg white in a mixing bowl and stir in the seasoning. Add the shredded fish to mix thoroughly.*
* *Heat the wok to bring 1 cup of the oil to boil then pour back into the oil container. Place the remaining 5 cups of oil into the wok over moderate heat. Put in the egg white mixture to cook for a while, turning every now and then. Remove and drain the egg white as soon as it floats.*
* *Heat the wok with the 2 tbsp of oil to sauté the ginger and spring onions. Sizzle the wine and pour in the stock to bring to the boil. Stir in the gravy mix to thicken the sauce. Return the egg white into the sauce to mix well. Remove and dish.*
* *Make a hole in the centre of the egg white to place in the egg yolk. Mix the sauce thoroughly and pour on top. Garnish with the sliced tomatoes then serve hot.*

白璧無瑕
Egg White with Shrimps

材料：

蝦仁6安（168克）
蛋白6隻
鹽½茶匙
胡椒粉少許
油6杯
羌茸½茶匙
葱粒½茶匙
火腿茸1湯匙
芫茜茸1湯匙

醃蝦料一鹽¼茶匙
　　　　生粉1茶匙
　　　　胡椒粉少許
　　　　蛋白1湯匙

調味料一酒1茶匙
　　　　上湯¼杯

餡料——生粉½茶匙
　　　　水1湯匙
　　　　胡椒粉少許
　　　　蔴油½茶匙

製法：

* 蝦挑腸洗淨抹乾水份，將醃料和勻加入放置一旁醃10分鐘。
* 蛋白打勻放入碗內加鹽、胡椒粉及蝦仁拌勻。
* 燒紅鑊加油1杯煮沸，搪勻鑊後將油傾回油桶內別用。另放入餘油5杯煮至微溫時停火，將蛋白及蝦仁放入油中泡至浮起。即可撈起隔淨餘油。鑊中餘下1湯匙油候用。
* 再燒熱鑊中油爆香羌、葱茸，潵酒加上湯煮沸。以生粉水打餡加入蔴油，將蛋白蝦仁重倒入鑊中兜勻上碟。
* 火腿及芫茜茸灑在上面點綴。

Ingredients:

6 oz (168 g) shelled shrimps
6 egg white
½ tsp salt
a pinch of pepper
6 cups corn oil
½ tsp minced ginger
½ tsp chopped spring onions
1 tbsp minced ham
1 tbsp minced parsley

Shrimp Marinade-   Seasoning-
¼ tsp salt   1 tsp wine
1 tsp cornflour   ¼ cup stock
a pinch of pepper
1 tbsp egg white

Gravy Mix-
½ tsp cornflour
1 tbsp water
a pinch of pepper
½ tsp sesame oil

Method:

* *Devein, wash and dry the shrimps. Coat with the marinade evenly and leave to stand for 10 minutes.*
* *Whisk the egg white in a mixing bowl then add the salt, pepper and the shrimps to mix well.*
* *Heat the wok with 1 cup of the oil then swirl and pour back into an oil container. Bring the other 5 cups of oil to just boil. Turn off the heat and pour in the egg white slowly to cook until it floats. Remove and drain, leaving about 1 tbsp oil in the wok for later use.*
* *Reheat the oil in the wok to sauté the ginger and spring onions. Sizzle the wine and add the stock to bring to boil. Thicken the sauce with the gravy mix and sesame oil. Return the egg and shrimps into the wok to toss evenly. Remove and dish.*
* *Sprinkle the ham and parsley on top to garnish.*

發財團圓
Fish Balls with Lettuce

材料：

魚肉1磅（½公斤）
髮菜¼安（7克）
沸水2杯
熟冬菇2隻
葱2棵
肥肉½安（14克）（隨意）
生粉¼杯
油4湯匙
生菜1磅（½公斤）

醃料—鹽½茶匙
糖½茶匙
胡椒粉少許
生粉1湯匙
水2湯匙
蔴油½茶匙

調味料－酒 1 茶匙
　　　　上湯 ¾ 杯
　　　　生抽 1 茶匙
　　　　糖 ½ 茶匙

饍料 —— 生粉 ½ 茶匙
　　　　水 1 湯匙
　　　　蔴油 ½ 茶匙

製法：

* 魚肉洗淨用布抹乾，切片剁爛成茸
  放入盆中。
* 髮菜洗淨浸透，放於 1 杯沸水中飛
  水。撈起沖凍隔乾水份切幼，加入
  魚茸中候用。
* 冬菇切幼粒。葱洗淨亦切幼粒。肥
  肉放入餘下沸水中飛水沖凍切幼粒
  。將所有粒及醃料一同放入魚茸中
  。
* 將醃料拌勻後用手撻至起膠，逐少
  將魚膠取出弄成小圓球，拍上少許
  生粉。
* 燒紅鑊加油 3 湯匙煮沸，將魚球放
  入半煎炸至微黃。取出隔去餘油。
  生菜洗淨候用。
* 再燒熱鑊加入餘油煮沸，灒酒加上
  湯，倒入魚球炆 8 分鐘。試妥味後
  再加生菜續煮 1 分鐘，以生粉水加
  蔴油埋饍，即可原鍋上桌。

Ingredients:

1 lb (½ kg) fish fillets
¼ oz (7 g) black moss
2 cups boiling water
2 cooked Chinese mushrooms
2 spring onions
½ oz (14 g) fat pork (optional)
¼ cup cornflour
4 tbsp corn oil
1 lb (½ kg) lettuce

Marinade-
½ tsp salt
½ tsp sugar
a pinch of pepper
1 tbsp cornflour
2 tbsp water
½ tsp sesame oil

Seasoning-
1 tsp wine
¾ cup stock
1 tsp light soy
½ tsp sugar

Gravy Mix-
½ tsp cornflour
1 tbsp water
½ tsp sesame oil

Method:

* *Wash and dry the fish fillets with
  a towel. Slice, mince and put in a
  mixing bowl.*
* *Wash and soak the black moss.
  Blanch for half a minute in 1 cup
  of the boiling water. Refresh,
  drain and chop finely. Mix into
  the fish purée.*
* *Dice the mushrooms. Wash and
  chop the spring onions. Blanch the
  fat pork in the remaining boiling
  water. Rinse and dice finely. Add
  into the fish purée with the marinade.*
* *Pound the fish purée until elastic.
  Shape the mixture into balls
  slightly smaller than a ping-pong
  then dredge with the cornflour.*
* *Heat the wok and bring 3 tbsp of
  the oil to the boil. Slide in the fish
  balls to shallow fry until light
  brown. Remove and drain. Wash
  the lettuce.*
* *Heat the casserole with the remaining oil. Sizzle the wine and
  pour in the stock. Add the fish
  balls to simmer for 8 minutes.
  Season to taste. Place the lettuce
  to cook for another minute.
  Thicken the juice with the gravy
  mix and sesame oil. Serve hot in
  the casserole.*

鰲頭獨佔
Fish Head Casserole

材料：

大魚頭1隻約1磅（½公斤）
生粉2湯匙
炸油3杯
熟冬菇4隻
粉皮2張
豆腐4件
紹菜8安（224克）

笋或紅蘿葡3安（84克）
沸水1杯
羗2片
葱3棵
油2湯匙

調味料－酒 1 茶匙
　　　　上湯 4 杯
　　　　鹽 $\frac{1}{4}$ 茶匙
　　　　生抽 2 湯匙
　　　　糖 2 茶匙
　　　　鷄粉 $\frac{1}{4}$ 茶匙
　　　　胡椒粉 $\frac{1}{4}$ 茶匙
　　　　蔴油 1 茶匙

製法：

* 魚頭洗淨抹乾後在內邊正中處輕斬一刀，以生粉塗勻。

* 燒紅鑊傾入炸油煮沸，滑入魚頭炸至金黃色，取出隔淨餘油。炸油留起候用。

* 冬菇片開。粉皮浸透切成小塊。豆腐每件開二放入以上炸油中炸至金黃色。

* 紹菜洗淨切開。笋或紅蘿蔔放入沸水中飛水，撈起沖凍切片。羌切絲。2 棵葱切度，餘下 1 棵切絲。

* 另鑊燒紅加油煮沸，爆香一半羌絲及葱度。讚酒加上湯轉倒入砂鍋內再煮沸。加入魚頭，冬菇片及紹菜文火煮 20 分鐘，再加其餘材料及調味料續煮 10 分鐘，以餘下羌葱絲灑面，即可原鍋上桌。

Ingredients:

1 fish head, about 1 lb (½ kg)
2 tbsp cornflour
3 cups oil for deep frying
4 cooked Chinese mushrooms
2 mung bean sheets
4 pieces bean curd
8 oz (224 g) cabbages
3 oz (84 g) bamboo shoots or carrots
1 cup boiling water
2 pieces ginger
3 spring onions
2 tbsp corn oil

Seasoning-

1 tsp wine
4 cups stock
¼ tsp salt
2 tbsp light soy
2 tsp sugar
¼ tsp chicken powder
¼ tsp pepper
1 tsp sesame oil

Method:

* *Wash and dry the fish head. Slash in the centre inside and open up to flatten slightly. Coat evenly with the cornflour.*

* *Heat the wok to bring the oil to the boil. Slide in the fish head to deep fry until golden brown. Remove and drain. Keep the hot oil for later use.*

* *Slice the mushrooms. Soak the mung bean sheets until softened and cut into small pieces. Halve each bean curd then deep fry in the above hot oil till golden.*

* *Clean and cut the cabbages. Blanch the bamboo shoots or carrots in the boiling water. Refresh, drain and slice. Shred the ginger and section 2 of the spring onions. Shred the third spring onion.*

* *Heat the wok and bring the oil to boil. Sauté half of the ginger and the sectioned spring onion till aromatic. Sizzle the wine and pour in the stock. Transfer into a casserole after it has been boiled. Add the fish head, mushrooms and cabbages to simmer over low heat for 20 minutes. Put in the other ingredients and seasoning to cook for another 10 minutes. Sprinkle the remaining shredded ginger and spring onion on top. Serve hot in the casserole.*

如魚得水

Fish in Hot and Sour Soup

材料：

黃花魚 1 條重 1 磅（½公斤）
炸油 2 杯
羌 3 片
葱 2 棵
油 1 湯匙
胡椒粒 2 茶匙
酒 1 湯匙
上湯 5 杯
鹽 2 茶匙
糖 2 茶匙
醋 2 湯匙
鷄粉 ½ 茶匙
蔴油 1 茶匙
胡椒粉少許
羌絲 1 湯匙
芫茜 3 棵
葱絲 1 湯匙

製法：

* 黃花魚打鱗劏開清除腸臟，洗淨抹乾水份。魚身每邊斜刀劃三條紋，每條紋相隔約 2 吋（5 公分）。
* 燒紅鑊傾入炸油煮沸，放入黃花魚炸片刻，取出隔去餘油。羌拍扁。葱切度。
* 另鑊燒熱加油 1 湯匙，爆香羌、葱度及胡椒粒。潛酒加上湯，滑入炸黃花魚煮 20 分鐘。隨即拌入鹽、糖、醋及鷄粉試妥味。
* 湯碗中放蔴油、胡椒粉、羌絲、芫茜及葱絲。將鍋內羌片及葱度棄去。全鍋連魚帶湯倒入碗中即可上桌熱食。

Ingredients:

1 lb (½ kg) yellow croaker
2 cups oil for deep frying
3 slices ginger
2 spring onions
1 tbsp corn oil for sautéeing
2 tsp pepper corns
1 tbsp wine
5 cups stock
2 tsp salt
2 tsp sugar
2 tbsp vinegar
½ tsp chicken powder
1 tsp sesame oil
a pinch of pepper
1 tbsp shredded ginger
3 parsley sprigs
1 tbsp shredded spring onions

Method:

* Scale, gut, wash and dry the fish with a towel. Crimp both sides at 2" (5 cm) intervals.
* Heat the wok to bring the oil to the boil. Put in the fish to deep fry for a while. Drain. Mash the ginger and section the spring onions.
* Heat the oil in the wok to sauté the ginger, spring onions and pepper corns till pungent. Sizzle the wine, add the stock and slide in the fish to simmer for 20 minutes. Stir in the salt, sugar, vinegar and chicken powder then adjust the flavor to taste.
* Put the sesame oil, pepper, shredded ginger, parsley and spring onions in the serving bowl and pour in the fish together with the soup. Discard the mashed ginger and spring onions then serve hot.

時来運到
Fish in Hot Iron Plate

材料：

鯇魚1條約2磅（1公斤）
羌6片
葱5棵
八角粉 ½ 茶匙
花椒粉 ½ 茶匙
油2湯匙
豬膏3安（84克）
沸水1杯

調味料－鹽1茶匙
　　　　糖2½茶匙
　　　　鷄粉½茶匙
　　　　生抽1茶匙
　　　　老抽1茶匙

製法：

* 鯇魚去腸臟後洗淨抹乾，保存魚鱗
  。
* 羌3片拍扁。葱2棵切度亦拍扁。
  用碗盛起加入調味料及2種香料撈
  勻，倒在魚上醃30分鐘。每隔10分
  鐘將魚反轉一次。
* 餘下羌片及葱拍扁，放在已預熱之
  烤盤中加油，將魚放在羌葱上。
* 豬膏放入沸水中洗淨，用毛巾抹乾
  後切絲蓋着整條魚。跟着將醃料淋
  在豬膏上。放入已預開375度（煤
  氣5度）焗爐內焗12分鐘。
* 焗妥之魚轉放在已預熱鐵碟上，將
  熱醃汁淋下即可上桌熱食。

Ingredients:

1 herring, about 2 lb (1 kg)
6 slices ginger
5 spring onions
½ tsp star anise powder
½ tsp xanthoxylum seed powder
2 tbsp corn oil
3 oz (84 g) pork fat
1 cup boiling water

Seasoning-
1 tsp salt
2½ tsp sugar
½ tsp chicken powder
1 tsp light soy
1 tsp dark soy

Method:

* Gut, clean and dry the fish with a
  towel. Retain the scales.
* Mash 3 pieces of the ginger.
  Section and mash 2 spring onions.
  Put the seasoning and the spices in
  a bowl then mix with the above
  ginger and spring onions. Pour on
  to the fish to marinate for 30
  minutes. Turn it over every 10
  minutes.
* Mash the remaining ginger and
  spring onions to put on to a preheated baking tray with the oil,
  then place the fish on top.
* Wash the pork fat with the boiling
  water. Dry with a towel then shred
  and cover the fish with it. Pour the
  marinade on the shredded fat
  and bake in a preheated 375 °F
  oven (Gas Mark 5) for 12 minutes.
* Transfer the baked fish on to
  a preheated iron plate. Pour the
  hot marinade on top and serve
  immediately.

金枝玉葉
Green Vegetables with Shredded Scallops

材料：

豆苗或菠菜1磅（½公斤）
瑤柱2安（56克）
水1杯
沸水4杯
油3湯匙
羌3片
葱2棵
葱頭1粒
蒜頭1粒

調味料－鹽¼茶匙
　　　　生抽1茶匙
　　　　糖1茶匙
　　　　酒1茶匙
　　　　瑤柱水½杯
　　　　蠔油1茶匙
　　　　胡椒粉少許

饙料──生粉1茶匙
　　　　水1湯匙
　　　　蔴油½茶匙

製法：

* 豆苗仔細洗淨摘妥。
* 瑤柱洗淨用水浸4小時後，置蒸籠
  內蒸30分鐘。隔乾水份撕成絲。瑤
  柱水留起作上湯用。
* 豆苗放於沸水中飛水30秒鐘，迅速
  倒起壓乾水份。
* 燒紅鑊加油2湯匙煮沸，灑鹽爆香
  羌、葱棄去。將豆苗倒入快手兜炒
  數下，加生抽及糖試妥味，盛在碟
  上。
* 另鑊燒熱加入餘油，爆香葱、蒜頭
  棄去，拌入瑤柱絲兜炒片刻。潸酒
  加上湯及餘下調味料煮5分鐘，即
  以生粉水加蠔油打饙，最後滴下蔴
  油兜勻淋在豆苗上。即可上桌。

Ingredients:

1 lb (½ kg) snow pea shoot or spinach
2 oz (56 g) dried scallops
1 cup water
4 cups boiling water
3 tbsp corn oil
3 slices ginger
2 spring onions
1 shallot
1 garlic clove

Seasoning-
¼ tsp salt
1 tsp light soy
1 tsp sugar
1 tsp wine
½ cup scallop water
1 tsp oyster sauce
a pinch of pepper

Gravy Mix-
1 tsp cornflour
1 tbsp water
½ tsp sesame oil

Method:

* Wash the spinach thoroughly and
  trim.
* Wash the scallops and soak in the
  water for 4 hours then steam for
  30 minutes. Drain and shred.
  Keep the water for later use.
* Pour the boiling water on to the
  spinach to scald for 30 seconds.
  Drain and squeeze out the excess
  water.
* Add 2 tbsp of the oil in the hot
  wok with the salt and sauté the
  ginger and spring onions until
  pungent then discard. Pour in the
  spinach to stir fry briskly. Season
  with the light soy and sugar. Remove on a platter.
* Heat another wok with the remaining oil to sauté the shallot
  and garlic then discard. Stir in the
  scallops to fry for a minute. Sizzle
  the wine, add the stock and seasoning to cook for 5 minutes.
  Trickle in the gravy mix with the
  oyster sauce. Sprinkle in the
  sesame oil then mask over the
  spinach. Dish and serve hot.

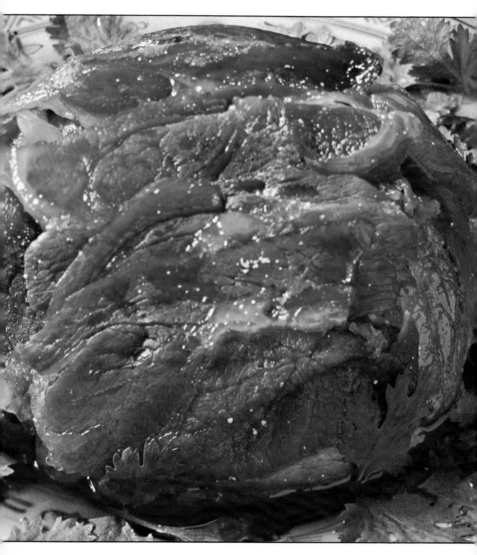

材料：

金華火腿½磅（224克）
熱水 1 杯
沸水 4 杯
蓮子 1 杯
菠蘿茸 1 杯

調味－冰糖碎 3 安（84克）
　　　紹酒 1 湯匙
　　　百花蜜 3 湯匙

製法：

* 火腿先用熱水洗擦乾淨。撈起再置
  2 杯沸水中焓30分鐘。取出洗淨隔
  乾水份去骨，切成長形薄片。
* 將火腿片排放在碗底及四週，零碎
  者放在上面。注入其餘 2 杯沸水後
  ，將整碗火腿放入蒸籠內蒸約20分
  鐘，取出隔去水份。
* 蓮子洗淨隔乾水份放在火腿上舖平
  。將菠蘿茸放在蓮子上，冰糖碎及
  紹酒拌勻後隨即淋下，重放入蒸籠
  內以猛火蒸 2 小時。
* 預備碟 1 隻，將整碗火腿覆扣在上
  ，倒去餘汁。將百花蜜淋在火腿上
  即成。

Ingredients:

½ lb (224 g) Virginia ham
1 cup hot water
4 cups boiling water
1 cup lotus seeds
1 cup mashed pineapple

Seasoning-
3 oz (84 g) mashed rock sugar
1 tbsp sherry
3 tbsp honey

Method:

* Place the ham in the hot water to
  trim the fat and clean thoroughly.
  Refresh and simmer in 2 cups of
  the boiling water for 30 minutes.
  Wash, drain and debone. Slice
  into oblong pieces.
* Arrange the sliced ham in a bowl
  and place the untidy pieces on top.
  Fill the bowl with the remaining
  boiling water then place in a
  steamer to cook for 20 minutes.
  Remove from the steamer and
  discard the water.
* Wash and drain the lotus seeds to
  place on top of the ham. Put the
  mashed pineapple on to the lotus
  seeds. Mix the sugar with the
  sherry then pour on top. Return it
  in the steamer and steam over high
  heat for 2 hours.
* Prepare a platter and turn the
  bowl on to it. Drain and pour the
  honey on the ham and serve hot.

四喜臨門
Jumbo Meatball Casserole (Lion's Head)

材料:

熟冬菇4隻
馬蹄10粒
上肉1磅(½公斤)
羌茸1湯匙
葱粒1湯匙
蛋1½隻
麵粉1湯匙
另麵粉1杯
水½杯
白菜12安(336克)
羌2片

葱2棵
炸油½鑊
油2湯匙

醃肉料－生抽2湯匙
　　　糖1湯匙
　　　酒2茶匙
　　　水3湯匙
　　　生粉2茶匙
　　　胡椒粉少許

調味－鹽½茶匙
　　　酒1茶匙
　　　上湯2杯
　　　生抽2茶匙
　　　糖1茶匙
　　　鷄粉¼茶匙
　　　胡椒粉少許

44

製法：

* 熟冬菇剁成茸。馬蹄去皮洗淨亦切幼。
* 上肉洗淨抹乾水份剁成肉茸。加入醃料中醃20分鐘。將全部材料與薑、葱茸及蛋1隻一同放入搞透。再篩入麵粉拌勻撻成肉醬，分成四等份。
* 另麵粉1杯篩在碟中，將四份肉醬分別放入拍上粉。餘下之粉則與另半隻蛋加水½杯開成粉漿。
* 白菜洗淨摘妥。薑切絲。葱切度。
* 燒紅鑊加入炸油煮至僅熱時，將肉糰置粉漿內拖勻放入沸油內炸之，邊炸邊以筷子撥開。炸至皮硬時即以罩籬撈起用壳輕拍上稍裂。重放油鍋內續炸至金黃色，撈起隔去餘油。
* 鑊中放油2湯匙煮沸。灑下鹽爆香薑，葱。倒入白菜兜炒½分鐘。讚酒加上湯再煮沸，調妥味後將獅子頭轉倒入砂窩內文火煮20分鐘即成。

Ingredients:

4 cooked Chinese mushrooms
10 water chestnuts
1 lb (½ kg) pork
1 tbsp minced ginger
1 tbsp chopped spring onions
1 ½ eggs
1 tbsp flour
1 extra cup plain flour
½ cup water
12 oz (336 g) Chinese cabbages
2 slices ginger
2 spring onions
½ wok corn oil for deep frying
2 tbsp corn oil for sautéeing

Pork Marinade-
2 tbsp light soy
1 tbsp sugar
2 tsp wine
3 tbsp water
2 tsp cornflour
a pinch of pepper

Seasoning-
½ tsp salt
1 tsp wine
2 cups stock
2 tsp light soy
1 tsp sugar
¼ tsp chicken powder
a pinch of pepper

Method:

* Mince the mushrooms. Peel, wash and chop the water chestnuts finely.
* Wash, dry and mince the pork. Immerse in the marinade for 20 minutes. Bind in the chopped ingredients, minced ginger and spring onion with an egg to mix well. Sift the flour into the mixture then pound firmly. Divide into 4 portions.
* Sift the other cup of flour in to a platter and dredge each meatball evenly. Blend the remaining flour with ½ an egg and the ½ cup of water to make a batter.
* Wash and trim the cabbages. Shred the ginger and section the spring onions.
* Heat the wok till hot, pour in the oil and bring to just boil. Coat the meatballs with the batter then slide in the oil to deep fry for 1 minute. Separate with a pair of chopsticks if they stick together. Remove with a strainer when it is crisp enough. Hit lightly with a scoop to form a crack on top of each. Return into the hot oil to deep fry till golden brown. Drain.
* Bring the 2 tbsp of oil to boil in the hot wok, sprinkle in the salt and sauté the ginger and spring onions until aromatic. Pour in the Chinese cabbages to stir fry for ½ a minute. Sizzle the wine and add the stock to bring to the boil. Season to taste. Transfer the meatballs into a casserole and simmer for 20 minutes. Serve hot in the casserole.

龍馬精神

Lobster in Spicy Sauce

材料：

龍蝦1隻約重2磅（1公斤）
生粉2湯匙
油4杯
羌2安（56克）
葱2安（56克）
葱頭2粒
蒜頭2粒
另油2湯匙

調味－酒1茶匙
　　　上湯1杯
　　　鹽½茶匙
　　　生抽1湯匙
　　　茄汁¼杯
　　　糖1湯匙
　　　辣油1茶匙
　　　醋數滴

製法：

* 龍蝦先用筷子1隻從尾部插入弄死
　，以清水仔細洗淨後，放在砧板上
　斬成大件。用刀將爪稍拍，放箸箕
　中灑下生粉拋勻。
* 燒紅鑊加入炸油煮至僅沸，將龍蝦
　件放入泡油至轉色。即可撈起隔去
　餘油。
* 羌、葱切絲。葱、蒜頭切片。
* 另鑊燒紅加油煮沸，爆香羌、葱絲
　各一半及葱蒜片，傾下龍蝦件猛火
　炒½分鐘。瓚酒加上湯再煮沸。試
　安味後蓋上鑊蓋煮3分鐘至上湯乾
　至尚餘少許，即灑入餘下羌葱絲兜
　勻上碟。嗜辣者可加紅椒絲2湯匙。

Ingredients:

1 lobster, about 2 lb (1 kg)
2 tbsp cornflour
4 cups corn oil
2 oz (56 g) ginger
2 oz (56 g) spring onions
2 shallots
2 garlic cloves
2 tbsp corn oil for sautéeing

Seasoning-
1 tsp wine
1 cup stock
½ tsp salt
1 tbsp light soy
¼ cup tomato ketchup
1 tbsp sugar
1 tsp chilli oil
a few drops vinegar

Method:

* *Insert a chopstick at the end of the lobster to kill it then wash thoroughly. Chop into serving pieces and crack the pincers lightly with a chopper. Toss evenly with the cornflour.*
* *Heat a wok and pour in the oil to bring to just boil. Slide in the lobster to parboil until the colour changes. Remove and drain.*
* *Shred the ginger and spring onions. Slice the shallots and garlic.*
* *Heat the wok with the oil. Sauté half of the ginger and spring onions, the garlic and shallots till pungent. Pour in the lobster to stir fry for half a minute. Sizzle the wine then add the stock to bring to the boil. Season to taste and cover with the lid to simmer for 3 minutes until the sauce is nearly dried. Scatter in the remaining ginger and spring onions to toss well. Dish and serve.*

春風得意
Meat Patties with Water Chestnuts

材料：

上肉1磅（½公斤）
馬蹄15粒
葱3棵
熟冬菇6隻
生粉¼杯
葱頭1粒
蒜頭1粒
油5湯匙
菠菜½磅（224克）

醃肉料—生抽2湯匙
糖1湯匙
酒1茶匙
胡椒粉少許
生粉1湯匙
水3湯匙
油2湯匙

調味料－酒 1 茶匙
　　　　上湯 ½ 杯
　　　　鹽 ¼ 茶匙
　　　　生抽 1 茶匙
　　　　糖 1 茶匙
　　　　雞粉 ¼ 茶匙
　　　　胡椒粉少許

饁料——生粉 1 茶匙
　　　　水 1 湯匙
　　　　蔴油 1 茶匙

製法：

* 上肉洗淨抹乾剁爛成茸。
* 馬蹄去皮洗淨磨爛成茸。
* 葱洗淨與冬菇皆切幼粒。
* 肉茸、馬蹄粒、葱粒及冬菇粒一同放於大盆中，倒入醃料搞透撻勻。然後用手將肉茸分成24等份，以生粉稍拍。
* 葱、蒜頭拍扁候用。
* 燒紅鑊加入油 2 湯匙煮沸，爆香葱、蒜頭棄去。將肉餅排在鑊中煎至兩面金黃色，取出盛起排放碟中。
* 菠菜仔細洗淨，放熱鑊中加油 2 湯匙略炒，盛起圍放在肉餅旁。
* 再燒熱鑊加入餘油煮沸，潽酒加上湯及調味料。試妥味後即以生粉水打饁淋在肉餅上。

Ingredients:

1 lb (½ kg) pork loin
15 water chestnuts
3 spring onions
6 cooked Chinese mushrooms
¼ cup cornflour
1 shallot
1 garlic clove
5 tbsp corn oil
½ lb (224 g) spinach

Pork Marinade-
2 tbsp light soy
1 tbsp sugar
1 tsp wine
a pinch of pepper
1 tbsp cornflour
3 tbsp water
2 tbsp corn oil

Seasoning-
1 tsp wine
½ cup stock
¼ tsp salt
1 tsp light soy
1 tsp sugar
¼ tsp chicken powder
a pinch of pepper

Gravy Mix-
1 tsp cornflour
1 tbsp water
1 tsp sesame oil

Method:

* *Wash, dry and mince the pork loin.*
* *Peel, wash and grate the water chestnuts.*
* *Wash and dice the spring onions with the mushrooms.*
* *Place the minced meat, water chestnuts, spring onions and mushrooms in a mixing bowl. Stir in the mixed marinade and pound till firm. Divide the mixture into 24 portions. Dredge in the cornflour to coat evenly.*
* *Mash the shallot and garlic.*
* *Heat the wok with 2 tbsp of the oil. Sauté the shallot and garlic till aromatic then discard. Arrange the meat patties in the wok to shallow fry till both sides are golden brown. Remove and dish.*
* *Wash the spinach thoroughly. Sauté in the hot wok with another 2 tbsp of oil then arrange round the meat patties.*
* *Reheat the wok with the remaining oil. Sizzle the wine, pour in the stock and season to taste. Thicken the sauce with the gravy mix. Mask over the patties and serve hot.*

好事齊来
Minced Dried Oyster with Diced Vegetables

材料：

蠔士4安（112克）
糖½茶匙
油3湯匙
瘦肉2安（56克）
溫油3杯
火腿2安（56克）
熟冬菇6隻
馬蹄6粒

榨菜1安（28克）
荷蘭豆2安（56克）
紅蘿蔔2安（56克）
沸水1杯
羗1片
葱頭2粒
芫茜1棵
生菜1磅（½公斤）

醃肉料－生抽½茶匙
糖¼茶匙
水1湯匙
生粉1茶匙
油1茶匙（後下）

調味—鹽 ¼ 茶匙　　　饋料—生粉 ½ 茶匙
　　　紹酒 1 茶匙　　　　　水 ½ 湯匙
　　　上湯 ¼ 杯　　　　　蔴油 1 茶匙
　　　生抽 1 茶匙
　　　蠔油 1 茶匙
　　　糖 1 茶匙
　　　胡椒粉少許

製法：

* 蠔士以清水浸30分鐘後洗淨，加入
  糖及油 1 湯匙拌勻。置蒸籠內蒸15
  分鐘，取出攤凍切成幼粒。
* 豬肉洗淨切粒將醃料和勻倒入醃10
  分鐘後，再加油續醃5分鐘。隨即
  放入溫油中泡油，取出隔淨餘油。
* 火腿、冬菇、馬蹄、榨菜及荷蘭豆
  皆切幼粒。
* 紅蘿蔔放於沸水中飛水，取出切幼
  粒。羌，葱頭剁爛。芫茜摘妥切粒
  。生菜洗淨放在碟旁候用。
* 燒紅鑊加入餘油煮沸，灑鹽放入羌
  、葱茸炒勻。將紅蘿蔔粒及荷蘭豆
  粒放入爆炒約20秒鐘後，即放入其
  餘各粒（芫茜除外）兜勻。讚酒加
  上湯試妥味，以生粉水加蔴油拌勻
  埋饋，灑下芫茜茸即成。
* 生菜跟上同食。

Ingredients:

4 oz (112 g) dried oyster
½ tsp sugar
3 tbsp corn oil
2 oz (56 g) lean pork
3 cups warm oil
2 oz (56 g) ham
6 cooked mushrooms
6 water chestnuts
1 oz (28 g) Szechuen preserved vegetable
2 oz (56 g) snow peas
2 oz (56 g) carrots
1 cup boiling water
1 slice ginger
2 shallots
1 parsley sprig
1 lb (½ kg) lettuce

Meat Marinade-
½ tsp light soy
¼ tsp sugar
1 tbsp water
1 tsp cornflour
1 tsp corn oil, to be added last

Seasoning-
¼ tsp salt
1 tsp sherry
¼ cup stock
1 tsp light soy
1 tsp oyster sauce
1 tsp sugar
⅛ tsp pepper

Gravy Mix-
½ tsp cornflour
½ tbsp water
1 tsp sesame oil

Method:

* *Soak the dried oysters for 30 minutes then wash. Season with the sugar and 1 tbsp of the oil. Steam for 15 minutes, leave to cool and chop finely.*
* *Wash, dice the pork and mix well with the marinade for 10 minutes then blend in the oil to marinate for another 5 minutes. Parboil in the warm oil and drain.*
* *Dice the ham, mushrooms, water chestnuts, preserved vegetable and the snow peas.*
* *Blanch the carrots in the boiling water and dice finely. Mince the ginger and shallots. Trim and chop the parsley. Wash and trim the lettuce. Arrange on to a side dish to use as wrapping.*
* *Heat the wok with the remaining oil. Sprinkle in the salt then slide in the ginger and shallot to fry well. Add the carrots and snow peas to sauté for 20 seconds then put in all the ingredients except the parsley to mix well. Sizzle the wine, pour in the stock and season to taste. Thicken the juice with the gravy mix and the sesame oil. Dish and scatter in the chopped parsley. Remove and dish.*
* *Serve the dish with the lettuce.*

長生不老
Multi-flavour Chicken

材料：

鶏腿 2 隻共重 1 磅（½公斤）
花生 1 杯
沸水 1 杯
青瓜粒 1 杯
羗茸 1 茶匙
葱粒 1 湯匙

醃鶏料—羗汁 1 湯匙
　　　　酒 1 湯匙
　　　　生抽 1 湯匙
　　　　糖 1 茶匙
　　　　鶏粉 ¼ 茶匙

調味 —— 糖 2 茶匙
　　　　生抽 2 茶匙
　　　　白酒 1 茶匙
　　　　蔴油 1 茶匙
　　　　米醋 ½ 茶匙
　　　　蔴醬 2 湯匙
　　　　豆瓣醬 1 茶匙
　　　　上湯 4 湯匙
　　　　花椒粉 1 茶匙
　　　　蒜茸 1 茶匙

製法：

* 鶏腿洗淨抹乾，加入醃料放置一旁醃30分鐘。轉置蒸籠內以猛火蒸12分鐘。取出去骨切成粗粒。
* 花生浸於沸水中半小時，撈起去衣。放入已預熱 225 度（煤氣¼度）焗爐內烘30分鐘至乾脆。
* 青瓜粒、熟鶏粒、花生、羗茸及葱粒一同放入大碗中。
* 將上述各調味同放於另一小碗中拌勻，倒入大碗中搞拌。轉盛另一平碟中即可上桌。

Ingredients:

2 chicken thighs, about 8 oz (224 g)
　each
1 cup peanuts
1 cup boiling water
1 cup diced cucumber
1 tsp minced ginger
1 tbsp chopped spring onions

Chicken Marinade-
1 tbsp ginger juice
1 tbsp wine
1 tbsp light soy
1 tsp sugar
¼ tsp chicken powder

Seasoning-
2 tsp sugar
2 tsp light soy
1 tsp white wine
1 tsp sesame oil
½ tsp rice vinegar
2 tbsp sesame paste
1 tsp chilli paste or broadbean paste
4 tbsp stock
1 tsp xanthoxylum powder
1 tsp minced garlic

Method:

* Wash and dry the chicken thighs. Immerse in the marinade and leave aside for 30 minutes. Steam over high heat for 12 minutes. Remove the bones and dice.
* Soak the peanuts in the boiling water for half an hour then remove the skin. Bake in a preheated 225 °F (Gas Mark ¼) oven for 30 minutes or until crisp.
* Place the diced cucumber, chicken, peanuts, ginger and spring onions into a mixing bowl.
* Mix all the seasoning well in a small bowl then blend into the diced ingredients to stir thoroughly. Remove on to a platter and serve cold.

材料：

羊肉2磅（1公斤）
蘿蔔6安（168克）
馬蹄10粒
羗4安（112克）
生蒜4條
葱頭2粒
蒜頭2粒
芫茜2棵
陳皮1方吋
生菜1棵
油2湯匙

調味－南乳2湯匙
　　　磨豉2湯匙
　　　酒1湯匙
　　　上湯4杯
　　　生抽1湯匙
　　　片糖2湯匙

製法：

* 羊肉洗淨斬件，置白鑊中烙乾。
* 蘿蔔刮去皮洗淨切大件。馬蹄去皮洗淨輕輕拍扁。
* 羗刮淨洗妥切厚件後拍扁。生蒜洗淨切度。葱蒜頭皆拍扁。
* 芫茜洗淨摘妥。陳皮浸透切絲。生菜洗淨候用。
* 燒紅鑊加油煮沸，爆香羗、葱、蒜棄去。拌入南乳及磨豉兜勻。傾入羊肉爆炒片刻。瓚酒加上湯再煮沸。轉置瓦鍋內加入馬蹄及陳皮炆40分鐘，將蘿蔔加入續煮30分鐘。拌入調味試妥後原保上桌。芫茜，生菜放入保內即可。

Ingredients:

2 lb (1 kg) mutton
6 oz (168 g) moolie
10 water chestnuts
4 oz (112 g) ginger
4 leeks
2 shallots
2 garlic cloves
2 parsley sprigs
1 sq. in. (2.5 cm²) tangerine peel
1 lettuce
2 tbsp corn oil

Seasoning-
2 tbsp fermented bean curd
2 tbsp ground bean paste
1 tbsp wine
4 cups stock
1 tbsp light soy
2 tbsp brown sugar

Method:

* *Wash and chop the mutton into serving pieces. Parch in a hot wok until quite dry.*
* *Scrape, wash and cut the moolie into big chunks. Peel and wash the water chestnuts.*
* *Scrape, wash and slice the ginger into thick pieces then mash slightly. Wash and section the leeks. Mash the shallots and garlic.*
* *Trim and chop the parsley. Soak and shred the tangerine peel. Wash the lettuce for later use.*
* *Heat the wok to bring the oil to the boil. Sauté the ginger, shallots and garlic till aromatic. Stir in the fermented beancurd and ground bean paste to mix well. Pour in the mutton to fry well. Sizzle the wine, add the stock to bring to boil. Transfer into a casserole, add the water chestnuts and tangerine peel to stew for 40 minutes. Put in the moolie to braise for another 30 minutes. Season to taste. Sprinkle in the parsley and add the lettuce to serve hot.*

龍鳳呈祥
Paper-wrapped Chicken and Prawns

材料：

鷄柳8安（224克）
蝦肉8安（224克）
玻璃紙一張
油2湯匙
葱6棵

紅蘿蔔2安（56克）
沸水1杯
芫茜2棵
炸油½鑊
紅蘿蔔絲1杯
生菜絲1杯

醃鷄料－羌粉 1 茶匙
　　　　五香粉 1 茶匙
　　　　酒 1 茶匙
　　　　生抽 1 湯匙
　　　　糖 1 茶匙
　　　　生粉 1 茶匙
　　　　水 2 湯匙
　　　　蔴油 1 茶匙

醃蝦料－羌汁 1 茶匙
　　　　生粉 1 茶匙
　　　　五香粉 ½ 茶匙
　　　　胡椒粉少許

製法：

* 鷄柳洗淨片成薄塊，將醃鷄料和勻倒入鷄柳中醃 20 分鐘。
* 蝦肉洗淨抹乾亦片成薄塊，將醃蝦料加入撈勻。
* 玻璃紙剪成 6 吋×6 吋（15 公分×15 公分）大小，每張紙內塗油。
* 葱洗淨切成 1 吋（2.5 公分）度。紅蘿蔔切片放入沸水中飛水，取出過冷河隔去水份切粗絲。芫茜洗淨摘妥。
* 將鷄一件放在玻璃紙一角，加葱度一撮在上向內包起，至鷄塊包完爲止。
* 蝦肉亦放在塗油玻璃紙一角，上放紅蘿蔔絲及芫茜，與鷄塊同樣包起。
* 燒紅鑊加油煮沸，將鷄包滑入沸油中炸 5 分鐘。隨放蝦包再炸 3 分鐘，撈起隔淨餘油排放在碟上。以芫茜絲及紅蘿蔔絲點綴上桌。

Ingredients:

8 oz (224 g) chicken fillet
8 oz (224 g) shelled prawns
1 sheet cellophane paper
2 tbsp corn oil
6 spring onions
2 oz (56 g) carrots
1 cup boiling water
2 parsley sprigs
½ wok oil for deep frying
1 cup shredded carrot
1 cup shredded lettuce

Chicken Marinade-
1 tsp ginger powder
1 tsp five-spice powder
1 tsp wine
1 tbsp light soy
1 tsp sugar
1 tsp cornflour
2 tbsp water
1 tsp sesame oil

Prawn Marinade-
1 tsp ginger juice
1 tsp cornflour
½ tsp five-spice powder
a pinch of pepper

Method:

* *Wash and slice the chicken into thin pieces. Immerse in the chicken marinade and leave aside for 20 minutes.*
* *Wash, dry and slice the prawns then dredge in the prawn marinade to coat evenly.*
* *Cut the cellophane paper into 6"x 6"(15 cm x 15 cm) squares. Grease each square with the oil.*
* *Wash and cut the spring onions into 1"(2.5 cm) sections. Slice and blanch the carrots in the boiling water. Refresh, drain and shred. Wash and trim the parsley.*
* *Place a piece of chicken on to the greased cellophane paper with some spring onions. Wrap up securely to form a packet.*
* *Put a piece of prawn on to a greased paper with the carrot and parsley on top. Seal up the same way as the chicken.*
* *Heat the wok and bring the oil to the boil. Slide in the meat packets and deep fry the chicken for 5 minutes and the prawns for 3 minutes. Remove and drain. Arrange on to a platter. Garnish with the parsley, shredded carrots and lettuce.*

丹鳳朝陽

Phoenix Cold Meat Combination

材料：

熟鷄胸肉 2 個
泡菜 1 磅 ($\frac{1}{2}$ 公斤)
熟冬菇10隻
鹵豬肝 $\frac{1}{2}$ 磅 (224克)
火腿 1 磅 ($\frac{1}{2}$ 公斤)
鮑魚 1 罐
鹵豬膶 $\frac{1}{2}$ 磅 (224克)
鹵鷄腎 $\frac{1}{2}$ 磅 (224克)
鹵豬肚 $\frac{1}{2}$ 磅 (224克)
紅蘿蔔 $\frac{1}{2}$ 隻
青瓜 1 條
熟鶉蛋 6 隻
車厘子數粒
青豆 1 湯匙
熟蝦 $\frac{1}{2}$ 磅 (224克)
海蜇 4 安 (112克)
芫茜數棵
蔴油 1 湯匙

製法：

* 鷄胸肉、泡菜及熟冬菇一隻切幼絲。預備大圓碟一個，以部份泡菜墊底，鷄絲舖面砌成鳳頭及頸，以冬菇絲作鳳眼。
* 另以部份泡菜墊底做成鳳身。豬肝、火腿、鮑魚及冬菇皆切片，分別排成四行作右翼，另以餘下各片排成三行作左翼。
* 鹵水腎切片排成長條作鳳尾。豬肚預先以重物壓扁後切片排放在鹵水腎側邊，兩側再排兩行長短不一之火腿片。
* 紅蘿蔔及青瓜亦切片作鳳尾之羽毛。將已切片之鶉蛋，車厘子及青豆粒分別放在每一片青瓜上。
* 熟蝦圍成一圓圈，中放海蜇絲以芫茜裝飾。灑下蔴油，上桌凍食。

Ingredients:

2 cooked chicken breasts
1 lb (½ kg) pickles
10 cooked Chinese mushrooms
½ lb (224 g) spicy liver
1 lb (½ kg) ham
1 tin abalone
½ lb (224 g) spicy tongue
½ lb (224 g) spicy gizzards
½ lb (224 g) spiced pig's stomach
½ carrot
1 cucumber
½ dozen cooked quails' eggs
a few cherries
1 tbsp sweet peas
½ lb (224 g) cooked shrimps
4 oz (112 g) jelly fish
a few parsley sprigs
1 tbsp sesame oil

Method:

* *Finely shred the chicken, pickled vegetables and 1 of the mushrooms. Prepare a large platter and place some pickled vegetables on to it then arrange the shredded chicken on the vegetables in the shape of a phoenix's head and neck. Use a shredded mushroom as the eye.*
* *Place a larger portion of pickled vegetables on the platter to form the phoenix's body. Slice and arrange the liver, ham, abalone and mushrooms in 4 rows to form the right wing. Arrange another 3 rows of the sliced tongue, abalone and mushrooms as its left wing.*
* *Slice the gizzard and arrange as the phoenix's tail. Press the spiced stomach with a heavy weight. Cut and arrange at the side of the sliced gizzards. Arrange a few pieces of ham at one side of the gizzards and another row at the side of the stomach.*
* *Slice the carrot and cucumber to place at the side of the tail to form the phoenix's feathers. Put the sliced quails' eggs, cherries and peas on to each piece of cucumber.*
* *Arrange the cooked shrimps in a circle and place the shredded jelly fish in the centre. Garnish with the trimmed parsley. Sprinkle the sesame oil on top and serve cold.*

拼盤製作過程
Procedure of preparing the Phoenix Combination

1. Put the pickled vegetables at one side of the plate.
   排放酸菜在大盤之一邊。

2. Shred the chicken breast finely. Arrange on the vegetables in the shape of a phoenix's neck. Cut a small piece of mushroom to resemble the eye.
   雞胸肉切幼絲，排放在酸菜上作鳳頸之幼毛，切冬菇絲作鳳眼。

3. Arrange the sliced liver, ham, abalone and mushrooms to form four rows as the phoenix's wing.
   將豬肝片、火腿片、鮑魚片及冬菇片排成四行作右翼。

4 ⇩

6 ⇧

5 ⇨

4. Arrange another three rows of sliced liver, abalone and mushrooms to resemble the left wing.

再將另一部份豬肝片、鮑魚片及冬菇片排成左翼。

5. Slice the spicy gizzards and arrange as the phoenix's tail.

將雞腎片砌成鳳尾。

6. Arrange the spicy stomach, sliced ham to complete the long tail.

另將鹵豬肚、火腿片分別排放腎片兩側。

嘻哈歡笑
Prawns in Tomato Sauce

材料：

大蝦 8 隻
沸水 2 杯
羌 2 片
葱 2 棵
蒜頭 2 粒
油 2 湯匙
生菜 ½ 磅（224克）

調味料一酒 ½ 湯匙
　　　　上湯 ¼ 杯
　　　　茄汁 3 湯匙
　　　　鹽 ¼ 茶匙
　　　　糖 1 茶匙
　　　　醋 1 茶匙

饡料 ——生粉 1 茶匙
　　　　水 1 湯匙
　　　　蔴油 1 茶匙
　　　　胡椒粉少許

製法：

* 大蝦用剪刀剪去蝦鬚及腳爪。挑腸洗淨用刀斜切成三段。
* 將蝦碎放在筲箕內，放入沸水略拖，取出隔去水份。
* 羌切絲。葱切度。蒜頭去衣切片。
* 燒紅鑊加油煮沸爆香羌絲及蒜片。潷酒倒入上湯再煮沸，加入茄汁、鹽、糖及醋和勻。試妥味後傾入蝦碎煮 3 分鐘，即以生粉和水拌勻慢慢流入和成饡，灑下蔴油及胡椒粉拋勻。
* 生菜洗淨抹乾水份舖在碟上，將蝦碎盛在中央即可上桌。

Ingredients:

8 large prawns
2 cups boiling water
2 slices ginger
2 spring onions
2 garlic cloves
2 tbsp corn oil
½ lb (224 g) lettuce

Seasoning-
½ tbsp wine
¼ cup stock
3 tbsp tomato ketchup
¼ tsp salt
1 tsp sugar
1 tsp vinegar

Gravy Mix-
1 tsp cornflour
1 tbsp water
1 tsp sesame oil
a pinch of pepper

Method:

* Trim and devein the prawns neatly. Wash and divide each prawn into three sections.
* Put the prawns in a strainer and scald with the boiling water. Drain.
* Shred the ginger and section the spring onions. Peel and slice the garlic.
* Heat the wok to bring the oil to the boil. Saute the giner and garlic till aromatic. Sizzle the wine, pour in the stock to bring to boil. Add the ketchup, salt, sugar and vinegar to mix well. Season to taste then slide in the prawns to simmer for 3 minutes. Mix the cornflour with the water then slowly stream into the sauce to thicken. Sprinkle in the sesame oil and pepper to toss well.
* Wash and arrange the lettuce on to the platter. Place the prawns in the centre and serve hot.

珠光寶氣
Quails' Eggs in Crab

材料：

大花蟹 1 隻約重 1 磅（ $\frac{1}{2}$ 公斤）
鵪蛋 6 隻
凍水 1 杯
油 2 湯匙
蛋白 2 隻
沸水 2 杯
薯仔 2 隻
青菜葉數片
炸油 $\frac{1}{2}$ 鑊
鹽 $\frac{1}{2}$ 茶匙

調味－酒 1 茶匙
　　　上湯 $\frac{1}{2}$ 杯
　　　鹽 $\frac{1}{4}$ 茶匙
　　　糖 $\frac{1}{2}$ 茶匙
　　　胡椒粉少許

饋料－生粉 $\frac{1}{2}$ 茶匙
　　　水 $\frac{1}{2}$ 湯匙
　　　蔴油 1 茶匙

製法：

* 大花蟹放水喉下擦去污漬冲洗乾淨。置蒸籠內猛火蒸約10分鐘，取出揭開蟹蓋，除去沙囊。將蟹腹內之蟹肉取出少許以小碟子盛起候用。
* 鵪蛋放入鍋中加凍水焓熟去殼。
* 燒紅鑊加油 2 湯匙，讚酒加上湯煮沸。倒入鵪蛋，調味料及蟹肉煮 3 分鐘，以生粉水打饋拌勻盛在蟹腹內，把蟹殼蓋上使其重新成爲原整之蟹。
* 蛋白放大碗中以蛋撥打至起泡，倒在沸水中稍煮。隔去水份，放在蟹口前使其看來像蟹吐出之白沫。
* 薯仔及菜葉皆切幼絲。另鑊燒熱加入炸油煮沸，放入薯絲及菜絲炸脆。隔去餘油，灑上鹽後圍放在蟹旁使成海草狀。

Ingredients:

1 crab, about 1 lb (½ kg)
6 quails' eggs
1 cup cold water
2 tbsp corn oil
2 egg whites
2 cups boiling water
2 potatoes
a few green vegetable leaves
½ wok oil for deep frying
½ tsp salt

Seasoning-
1 tsp wine
½ cup stock
¼ tsp salt
½ tsp sugar
a pinch of pepper

Gravy Mix-
½ tsp cornflour
½ tbsp water
1 tsp sesame oil

Method:

* Scrub and wash the crab under a running tap. Place in a steamer and cook for 10 minutes over high heat. Remove the shell and discard the inedible parts. Take a little crab meat aside for making the gravy.
* Boil the quails' eggs in the cold water and shell.
* Heat the wok with the 2 tbsp of oil. Sizzle the wine and add the stock to bring to the boil. Stir in the quails' eggs, seasoning and crab meat to simmer for 3 minutes. Blend in the gravy mix to thicken, then pour into the crab. Replace the shell of the crab to form its original shape.
* Whisk the egg whites in a large bowl till fluffy. Pour into the boiling water to cook for a while and drain. Place in front of the crab to make it look like a crab spitting out bubbles.
* Shred the potatoes and vegetables finely. Heat the wok and bring the oil to the boil to deep fry the potatoes and vegetable until crisp. Drain and sprinkle the salt on top to mix well. Arrange round the crab as garnishing.

積福積善
Rice Crisps with Assorted Meat

材料：

鮑魚3片
火腿3片
熟鷄肉2件
熟冬菇4隻
鷄腎2隻
豬肚1塊
蝦仁½杯
沸水3杯

笋或紅蘿蔔2安（56克）
青豆½杯
飯1杯
炸油½鑊

醃腎料－酒1茶匙
　　　　羗汁1茶匙
　　　　生粉1茶匙

醃蝦料－蛋白1茶匙
　　　　胡椒粉少許
　　　　生粉1茶匙

調味－酒 1 茶匙　　饡料－生粉 3 湯匙
　　　上湯 3 杯　　　　　水 2 湯匙
　　　鹽 ¼ 茶匙　　　　老抽 ¼ 茶匙
　　　生抽 1 茶匙　　　　蔴油 1 茶匙
　　　鷄粉 ¼ 茶匙
　　　糖 1½ 茶匙
　　　胡椒粉少許

製法：

* 鮑魚片、火腿、鷄肉及冬菇切丁候
  用。
* 鷄腎及豬肚亦切丁加入醃腎料中醃
  15分鐘。
* 蝦仁加蛋白，胡椒粉及生粉撈勻，
  與鷄腎及豬肚一同放於 2 杯沸水中
  飛水，取出過冷河隔乾水份。
* 紅蘿蔔切丁與青豆放入餘下沸水中
  飛水，撈起冲凍隔乾水份。
* 飯放在塗油焗盆中壓實成一片，轉
  置已預熱 300 度（煤氣 2 度）焗爐
  內焗至金黃色。取出弄成數件後放
  入沸油中炸至金黃及鬆起，放入大
  碗中。炸油倒回油桶內只餘 2 湯匙
  留在鑊中。
* 燒沸鑊中油，濳酒加入上湯，隨即
  拌入雜錦粒煮片刻。調妥味後以生
  粉水埋饡。將雜錦料倒在炸飯焦上
  。即可供食。

Ingredients:

3 slices abalone
3 slices ham
2 pieces cooked chicken
4 cooked Chinese mushrooms
2 chicken gizzards
1 piece pig's stomach
½ cup shelled shrimps
3 cups boiling water
2 oz (56 g) bamboo shoots or carrots
½ cup sweet peas
1 cup cooked rice
½ wok boiling oil for deep frying

Gizzard Marinade-　Shrimp Marinade-
1 tsp wine　　　　1 tsp egg white
1 tsp ginger juice　a pinch of pepper
1 tsp cornflour　　1 tsp cornflour

Seasoning-
1 tsp wine
3 cups stock
¼ tsp salt
1 tsp light soy
¼ tsp chicken powder
1½ tsp sugar
a pinch of pepper

Gravy Mix-
3 tbsp cornflour
2 tbsp water
¼ tsp dark soy
1 tsp sesame oil

Method:

* Dice the abalone, ham, chicken
  and mushrooms.
* Dice and mix the gizzards and
  stomach with the marinade for 15
  minutes.
* Coat the shrimps with the egg
  white, pepper and cornflour
  evenly. Blanch in 2 cups of the
  boiling water with the gizzards
  and stomach then refresh and
  drain.
* Dice and blanch the carrot with
  the sweet peas in the remaining
  cup of boiling water. Refresh and
  drain.
* Place the cooked rice on a greased
  baking tray and press firmly. Bake
  in the preheated 300 °F (Gas Mark
  2) oven until golden. Remove and
  break into a few pieces. Bring the
  oil to the boil in the wok and deep
  fry the rice pieces to form rice
  crisps. Place the rice crisps into a
  big bowl and pour the oil back into
  the oil container, leaving about 2
  tbsp in the wok.
* Reboil the oil in the wok then
  sizzle the wine and add the stock.
  Stir in all the diced ingredients to
  simmer for a minute. Season to
  taste and thicken the sauce with
  the gravy mix. Pour over the rice
  crisps and serve immediately.

红皮赤壮
Roast Suckling Pig Hors D'oeuvre

材料：

海蜇 4 安（112克）
沸水 2 杯
蔴油 1 茶匙
生抽 1 茶匙
火腿 4 安（112克）
鹵棼蹄 4 安（112克）
鹵豬肚 4 安（112克）
鹵鷄腎 3 隻
鹵豬脷 1 條
鹵牛腱 1 條
皮蛋 4 隻
乳豬 1 磅（½公斤）
菠蘿 2 片
車厘子數粒
芫茜數棵

製法：

* 海蜇切幼絲洗淨。將海蜇放入沸水
  中燙30秒鐘。撈起置水喉下沖 1 小
  時後，揸乾水份用蔴油及生抽撈勻
  調妥味放在長碟中央。
* 火腿，棼蹄，豬肚，鷄腎，豬脷及
  牛腱全部切薄片。分別環繞海蜇排
  放四週。
* 皮蛋去殼亦切片，環繞海蜇排放雜
  肉片之上。
* 乳豬斬件，排放在海蜇之上。
* 將菠蘿片，車厘子及芫茜分別伴放
  碟旁點綴。即可上桌。

Ingredients:

4 oz (112 g) jelly fish
2 cups boiling water
1 tsp sesame oil
1 tsp light soy
4 oz (112 g) ham
4 oz (112 g) stuffed trotter
4 oz (112 g) spicy stomach
3 spicy chicken gizzards
1 spicy tongue
1 spicy shin
4 thousand-year eggs
1 lb (½ kg) roast suckling pig
2 slices pineapple
a few cherries
a few parsley sprigs

Method:

* Shred and wash the jelly fish.
  Bring the water to the boil and
  scald the jelly fish for 30 seconds.
  Refresh under a running tap for 1
  hour. Drain and season with the
  sesame oil and light soy. Place in
  the centre of a platter.
* Slice the ham, trotter, stomach,
  gizzard, tongue and the shin.
  Arrange these various types of
  meat around the jelly fish.
* Shell and section the thousand-
  year eggs. Place on to the meat to
  surround the jelly fish.
* Chop the suckling pig into neat
  pieces and place on top of the jelly
  fish.
* Garnish the dish with the pineapple, cherries and parsley sprigs.

鴛鴦新巢
Sautéed Eel with Assorted Vegetables

材料：

幼麵2安（56克）
沸水2杯
粉絲2安（56克）
炸油½鑊
鰻魚1條約20安（560克）
草菰4安（112克）
芥蘭4安（112克）
珍珠筍4安（112克）
紅蘿蔔2安（56克）

熟冬菇4隻
羌2片
葱頭2粒
蒜頭2粒
油2湯匙

醃魚料—生抽1湯匙
　　　糖1茶匙
　　　胡椒粉少許
　　　生粉1湯匙
　　　蒜茸1湯匙

調味—鹽½茶匙
　　　糖1茶匙
　　　酒1湯匙
　　　上湯½杯
　　　蠔油1湯匙
　　　胡椒粉⅛茶匙

饡料—生粉1茶匙
　　　水1湯匙
　　　蔴油1茶匙

70

製法：

* 幼麵放沸水中飛水，撈起過冷河隔
  乾水份，沸水留起候用。粉絲用水
  浸軟，隔去水份。將幼麵放在罩籬
  中，麵上再放上另一隻罩籬，隨即
  放入沸油中炸脆至變金黃色，取出
  隔淨餘油。粉絲亦放罩籬中置沸油
  同樣炸之。將炸油傾回油桶內攤凍。
* 鰻魚去腸臟及起肉切骨牌，拌入醃
  料放置一旁醃20分鐘。
* 炸油重傾回熱鑊中，將鰻魚放入泡
  油2分鐘，取出盛起隔去油。
* 草菇洗淨剪妥。芥蘭，珍珠筍，紅
  蘿蔔及冬菇皆切粒，一同放於以上
  沸水中飛水，撈起沖凍隔乾水份。
* 羗切絲。葱蒜頭剁茸。
* 鑊洗淨再燒熱加油煮沸，灑下鹽爆
  香羗葱蒜。將雜菜粒倒入加糖炒 ½
  分鐘。倒入鰻魚兜勻。潷酒加上湯
  試至合味，即以生粉水埋獻，灑下
  蔴油再拋勻。即可倒在幼麵及粉絲
  籃內上桌。

Ingredients:

2 oz (56 g) cake noodles
2 cups boiling water
2 oz (56 g) bean threads
½ wok hot oil for deep frying
1 eel, about 20 oz (560 g)
4 oz (112 g) straw mushrooms
4 oz (112 g) broccoli
4 oz (112 g) baby corns
2 oz (56 g) carrots
4 cooked Chinese mushrooms
2 slices ginger
2 shallots
2 garlic cloves
2 tbsp corn oil

Fish Marinade-
1 tbsp light soy
1 tsp sugar
a pinch of pepper
1 tbsp cornflour
1 tbsp minced garlic

Seasoning-
½ tsp salt
1 tsp sugar
1 tbsp wine
½ cup stock
1 tbsp oyster sauce
1/8 tsp pepper

Gravy Mix-
1 tsp cornflour
1 tbsp water
1 tsp sesame oil

Method:

* *Blanch the noodles in the boiling
  water, refresh and drain. Keep the
  water for later use. Soak the bean
  threads until softened then drain.
  Place the noodles loosely in one
  strainer and press with another to
  shape into a basket. Deep fry in
  the hot oil till crisp and golden.
  Drain. Deep fry the bean threads
  as well. Pour the oil back into the
  container and leave to cool.*
* *Gut, debone and cut the eel into
  bite-sized pieces. Mix with the
  marinade and leave to stand for 20
  minutes.*
* *Return the oil into the heated wok
  to parboil the eel for 2 minutes
  when the oil is just warm. Remove
  and drain.*
* *Clean and trim the straw mushrooms. Cut the broccoli, baby
  corns, carrots and mushrooms
  into bite-sized pieces. Blanch in
  the above boiling water, refresh
  and drain.*
* *Shred the ginger. Mince the
  shallots and garlic.*
* *Clean and reheat the wok to bring
  the oil to the boil. Sprinkle in the
  salt. Sauté the ginger, shallots and
  garlic till aromatic. Add the as-
  sorted vegetables with the sugar to
  fry for half a minute. Pour in the
  eel to mix well. Sizzle the wine,
  add the stock and season to taste.
  Stir in the gravy mix and drop in
  the sesame oil to toss well. Spoon
  into the noodles and bean thread
  baskets to serve hot. Garnish with
  the deep fried vegetable leaves,
  tomatoes and lemon.*

仙姬送子
Sautéed Scallops with Celery

材料：

帶子1磅（½公斤）
鹽1茶匙
生粉1茶匙
紅蘿蔔2安（56克）
芥蘭½磅（224克）
沸水2杯
羗¼安（7克）
葱頭1粒

蒜頭1粒
葱3棵
油3杯作泡油用
另油2湯匙

醃帶子料－羗汁1湯匙
　　　　　生粉1湯匙

調味料—鹽 ¼ 茶匙
　　　　紹酒 1 茶匙
　　　　上湯 ¼ 杯
　　　　蠔油 1 茶匙
　　　　糖 ½ 茶匙
　　　　胡椒粉少許

饢料 —— 生粉 ½ 茶匙
　　　　水 ½ 湯匙
　　　　蔴油 ½ 茶匙

製法：

* 帶子用鹽及生粉洗淨污垢後，以清
　水沖淨隔乾水份，加入醃料放置一
　旁醃20分鐘。
* 紅蘿蔔切片。芥蘭洗淨摘妥後與紅
　蘿蔔一同放入沸水中飛水。
* 羗切絲。葱蒜頭切片。葱切度。
* 燒紅鑊加油煮至微溫時轉爲慢火，
　將帶子傾入泡油約30秒鐘，撈起隔
　去餘油。
* 另鑊燒熱加油 2 湯匙煮沸。灑下鹽
　爆香羗、葱、蒜，隨即傾入芥蘭及
　紅蘿蔔猛火炒 1 分鐘。濆酒加上湯
　試妥味後，滑入帶子兜勻。即以生
　粉水埋饢，再灑下蔴油及葱度即可
　上碟。

Ingredients:

1 lb (½ kg) fresh scallops
1 tsp salt
1 tsp cornflour
2 oz (56 g) carrot
½ lb (224 g) broccoli
2 cups boiling water
¼ oz (7 g) ginger
1 shallot
1 garlic clove
3 spring onions
3 cups corn oil for parboiling
2 tbsp corn oil

Scallop Marinade-
1 tbsp ginger juice
1 tbsp cornflour

Seasoning-
¼ tsp salt
1 tsp cooking sherry
¼ cup stock
1 tsp oyster sauce
½ tsp sugar
a pinch of pepper

Gravy Mix-
½ tsp cornflour
½ tbsp water
½ tsp sesame oil

Method:

* *Clean the scallops thoroughly
with the salt and cornflour. Refresh and drain. Mix well with the
marinade then leave aside for 20
minutes.*
* *Slice the carrot. Wash, trim and
blanch the broccoli in the boiling
water with the carrot.*
* *Shred the ginger. Slice the shallot
and garlic. Section the spring
onions.*
* *Heat the wok and bring the oil to
just boil over low heat. Slide in the
scallops to parboil for 30 seconds.
Remove and drain.*
* *Bring the 2 tbsp of oil in the wok
to boil then sprinkle in the salt.
Add the ginger, shallot and garlic
then stir in the broccoli and carrot
to sauté for a minute. Sizzle the
wine, add the stock and season to
taste. Slide in the scallops to mix
thoroughly. Thicken the sauce
with the gravy mix. Drop in the
sesame oil and garnish with the
sectioned spring onions. Dish and
serve hot.*

花團錦簇

Sautéed Shrimps with Cashew Nuts

材料：

蝦肉8安（224克）
溫油4杯
腰果4安（112克）
沸水3杯
鹽1湯匙
椰菜花4安（112克）
青椒2安（56克）
紅椒1安（28克）
紅蘿蔔1安（28克）

羌1片
葱頭1粒
蒜頭1粒
油2湯匙

醃蝦料－蛋白½隻
生粉1茶匙
胡椒粉少許

調味―鹽¼茶匙
　　海鮮醬½湯匙
　　磨豉½湯匙
　　酒1茶匙
　　水2湯匙
　　生抽1茶匙
　　糖½茶匙
　　蔴油1茶匙

製法：

* 蝦肉挑腸洗淨抹乾，放入和勻之醃料中醃10分鐘後。滑下溫油中泡油。撈起隔淨。將油盛起放置一旁攤凍候用。
* 腰果放入沸水中加鹽焓2分鐘，取出隔去水份吹乾。鹽水留起候用。
* 鑊燒熱加入以上攤凍之油，即將腰果放入以文火炸至轉爲金黃色。以罩籬撈起隔去餘油。
* 椰菜花切丁。靑、紅椒去籽與紅蘿蔔一同切粒。
* 椰菜花及紅蘿蔔粒放入上述鹽水中飛水。撈起沖淨隔乾水份。羗切絲。葱、蒜頭切片。
* 另鑊燒紅加油煮沸，灑下鹽爆香羗絲及葱、蒜片。將鑊提起加入海鮮醬及磨豉，倒入雜菜粒及蝦仁迅速炒勻。潷酒拌入已和勻之調味料拌炒。最後滴下蔴油及再加腰果拋勻，即可上碟。

Ingredients:

8 oz (224 g) shelled shrimps
4 cups warm oil
4 oz (112 g) cashew nuts
3 cups boiling water
1 tbsp salt
4 oz (112 g) cauliflower
2 oz (56 g) capsicum
1 oz (28 g) chillies
1 oz (28 g) carrot
1 slice ginger
1 shallot
1 garlic clove
2 tbsp corn oil

Shrimp Marinade-
½ egg white
1 tsp cornflour
a pinch of pepper

Seasoning-
¼ tsp salt
½ tbsp Hoi Sin paste
½ tbsp ground bean paste
1 tsp wine
2 tbsp water
1 tsp light soy
½ tsp sugar
1 tsp sesame oil

Method:

* *Devein, wash and dry the shrimps. Mix well with the marinade the leave aside for 10 minutes. Parboil in the warm oil and drain. Leave the oil to cool for later use.*
* *Blanch the cashew nuts in the boiling water with the salt for 2 minutes. Remove and drain. Retain the boiling water*
* *Heat the wok and pour in the above cool oil. Slide in the nuts while the oil is still cool. Deep fry over low heat till light brown. Remove and drain on a kitchen paper.*
* *Cut the cauliflower into cubes. Deseed and dice the capsicum and chillies with the carrot.*
* *Blanch the cauliflower and carrot in the above salted water. Refresh and drain. Shred the ginger. Slice the shallot and garlic.*
* *Heat the oil in the wok and sprinkle in the salt. Sauté the ginger, shallot and garlic until aromatic. Remove the wok from the heat for a while to add the Hoi Sin and ground bean paste. Pour in the diced ingredients and the shrimps to fry rapidly. Sizzle the wine and stir in the mixed seasoning. Drop in the sesame oil and add the nuts to toss thoroughly. Dish and serve hot.*

金碧輝煌
Sautéed Shrimps with Diced Vegetables

材料：

蝦1磅（½公斤）
粗鹽1湯匙
生粉1湯匙
油2杯作泡油用
芥蘭2安（56克）
馬蹄2安（56克）
紅蘿蔔2安（56克）
水1杯

鹽1茶匙
糖1茶匙
粟米½杯
紅椒1隻
熟冬菇3隻
葱頭1粒
蒜頭1粒
油2湯匙

醃料－生粉1茶匙
胡椒粉少許
蛋白1隻

調味－鹽 ¼ 茶匙
　　　酒 1 茶匙
　　　上湯 ¼ 杯
　　　生抽 1 茶匙
　　　雞粉 ¼ 茶匙
　　　糖 ½ 茶匙
　　　胡椒粉少許

饋料－生粉 ½ 茶匙
　　　水 1 湯匙
　　　蔴油 1 茶匙

製法：

* 蝦去殼挑腸，灑粗鹽及生粉拋勻，
  置水喉下沖洗乾淨。以毛巾抹乾後
  ，放入和勻之醃料中略醃。
* 燒紅鑊加油煮至微溫，倒下蝦肉泡
  油至半熟，取出隔淨餘油。
* 芥蘭摘妥切粒。馬蹄去皮洗淨與紅
  蘿蔔一同切粒。水 1 杯煮沸加入鹽
  及糖，傾入芥蘭、馬蹄、紅蘿蔔粒
  及粟米飛水 1 分鐘。撈起沖凍隔去
  水份。
* 紅椒去籽與冬菇一同切粒。葱、蒜
  頭皆拍扁。
* 另鑊燒熱加油煮沸，灑鹽爆香葱、
  蒜頭棄去。隨即倒入雜菜兜炒約 1
  分鐘，加入蝦肉潷酒，傾入上湯及
  調味料再兜勻。試妥味後以生粉水
  埋饋。最後拌入蔴油即可上碟。

Ingredients:

1 lb (½ kg) shrimps
1 tbsp coarse salt
1 tbsp cornflour
2 cups corn oil for parboiling
2 oz (56 g) broccoli
2 oz (56 g) water chestnuts
2 oz (56 g) carrot
1 cup water
1 tsp salt
1 tsp sugar
½ cup sweet corn
1 chilli
3 cooked Chinese mushrooms
1 shallot
1 garlic clove
2 tbsp corn oil

Marinade-
1 tsp cornflour
a pinch of pepper
1 egg white

Seasoning-
¼ tsp salt
1 tsp wine
¼ cup stock
1 tsp light soy
¼ tsp chicken powder
½ tsp sugar
a pinch of pepper

Gravy Mix-
½ tsp cornflour
1 tbsp water
1 tsp sesame oil

Method:

* *Shell and devein the shrimps.
  Sprinkle the coarse salt and cornflour on to them then wash under
  a running tap. Dry with a towel.
  Mix well with the marinade.*
* *Heat the wok to bring the oil to
  just warm. Pour in the shrimps to
  parboil till half cooked. Remove
  and drain.*
* *Trim and dice the broccoli. Peel,
  wash and dice the water chestnuts
  and carrot. Bring the water to the
  boil with the salt and sugar. Slide
  in the broccoli, water chestnuts,
  carrot and the sweet corn to
  blanch for 1 minute. Refresh and
  drain.*
* *Deseed and dice the chilli and the
  mushrooms. Mash the shallot and
  garlic.*
* *Heat the wok to bring the oil to the
  boil then sprinkle in the salt. Place
  in the shallot and garlic to sauté
  and discard. Pour in the diced ingredients and sweet corn to fry for
  a minute. Add the shrimps and
  sizzle the wine. Pour in the stock
  and adjust the flavour to taste.
  Thicken the stock with the gravy
  mix and stir in the sesame oil to
  toss well. Dish and serve.*

普天同慶
Shark's Fin with Assorted Meat

材料：

酒2湯匙
水8杯
羌4片
葱頭4粒
急凍魚翅1磅（½公斤）
鷄肉4安（112克）
溫油3杯
瘦肉2安（56克）
火腿4安（112克）

熟冬菇4隻
笋4安（112克）
沸水1杯作飛水用
油2湯匙

醃鷄料－羌汁1茶匙
　　　　酒1茶匙
　　　　生粉1茶匙
　　　　蛋白½隻

醃肉料－生抽½茶匙
　　　　糖¼茶匙
　　　　酒½茶匙
　　　　水2茶匙
　　　　胡椒粉少許
　　　　生粉½茶匙

調味—酒 1 湯匙　　饋料—生粉 4 湯匙
　　　上湯 6 杯　　　　　水 ⅓ 杯
　　　鹽 1 茶匙　　　　　老抽 ½ 茶匙
　　　生抽 1 湯匙　　　　胡椒粉少許
　　　糖 1 茶匙　　　　　蔴油 1 茶匙

製法：

* 燒紅鑊，潷酒 1 湯匙，倒入清水 4
  杯。加薑 2 片及葱頭 2 粒煮沸。將
  魚翅放入以文火煮20分鐘以去腥味
  ，取出過冷河隔乾水份。薑，葱頭
  棄去。重複一次。
* 鷄切絲，放入醃鷄料中醃10分鐘後
  ，倒入溫油中泡片刻。隔淨餘油。
  將油盛起略攤凍候用。
* 瘦肉切絲，將醃肉料和勻倒入瘦肉
  中醃10分鐘。放入以上之溫油中泡
  油隔去餘油。
* 火腿及冬菇切絲。筍放入沸水中飛
  水，撈起沖凍切絲。
* 燒紅鑊加油，潷酒倒入上湯煮沸。
  將魚翅加入煮 1 小時。拌入其餘材
  料續煮10分鐘。將調味料和勻試妥
  味後，以生粉水和成濃度適中之湯
  即成。食時可加浙醋。

Ingredients:

2 tbsp wine
8 cups water
4 slices ginger
4 shallots
1 lb (½ kg) frozen shark's fin
4 oz (112 g) chicken meat
3 cups warm oil for parboiling
2 oz (56 g) lean pork
4 oz (112 g) ham
4 cooked Chinese mushrooms
4 oz (112 g) bamboo shoots
1 cup boiling water for blanching
2 tbsp corn oil

Chicken Marinade-
1 tsp ginger juice
1 tsp wine
1 tsp cornflour
½ egg white

Pork Marinade-
½ tsp light soy
¼ tsp sugar
½ tsp wine
2 tsp water
a pinch of pepper
½ tsp cornflour

Seasoning-
1 tbsp wine
6 cups stock
1 tsp salt
1 tbsp light soy
1 tsp sugar

Gravy Mix-
4 tbsp cornflour
⅓ cup water
½ tsp dark soy
a pinch of pepper
1 tsp sesame oil

Method:

* Heat the wok till very hot and
  sizzle in 1 tbsp of the wine then
  pour in 4 cups of the water. Add 2
  slices of the ginger and 2 shallots
  to bring to the boil. Put in the
  shark's fin to simmer over low
  heat for 20 minutes to get rid of the
  stale odour. Remove, refresh and
  drain. Discard the ginger and
  shallots. Repeat the process once
  more.
* Shred the chicken and soak in the
  marinade for 10 minutes. Parboil
  in the warm oil and drain. Leave
  the oil to cool and keep it for later
  use.
* Shred the pork and blend in the
  pork marinade to leave for 10
  minutes. Parboil in the above
  warm oil then drain.
* Shred the ham and the
  mushrooms. Blanch the bamboo
  shoots in the boiling water, refresh
  and shred.
* Heat the saucepan with the oil.
  Sizzle the wine and pour in the
  stock. Add the shark's fin to
  simmer for an hour then stir in the
  other ingredients and continue to
  cook for another 10 minutes.
  Adjust the flavour to taste and
  thicken the soup with the gravy
  mix. Serve hot with red vinegar.

固若金湯
Shark's Fin with Salted Egg Yolk

材料：

酒 2 湯匙
水 8 杯
羌 6 片
葱頭 6 粒
急凍魚翅 1 磅（½ 公斤）
鹹蛋 6 隻
上湯 6 杯
油 1 湯匙
火腿茸 1 湯匙
芫茜茸 1 茶匙
饅頭 3 個
炸油 4 杯

調味―酒 1 湯匙　　　饡料―生粉 4 湯匙
　　　鹽 1 茶匙　　　　　水 ⅓ 杯
　　　生抽 1 茶匙　　　麻油 ½ 茶匙
　　　糖 ½ 茶匙
　　　鷄精 ½ 粒
　　　胡椒粉 ⅛ 茶匙

製法：

* 燒紅鑊，灒酒倒入清水 4 杯，將羌片及葱頭各一半加入煮沸。魚翅放入煮 20 分鐘。取出魚翅，將羌及葱頭棄去。重覆以上做法一次。

* 鹹蛋焓 3 分鐘後放在水喉下冲凍去殼，除去蛋白。將 6 個鹹蛋黃放在搞拌器中，加入上湯 1 杯打至完全溶化成濃漿。

* 鍋燒熱加油煮沸，灒酒加入其餘上湯 5 杯，將魚翅放入煮 30 分鐘。拌入蛋黃混合物及調味料續煮 10 分鐘，以生粉水埋饡。火腿及芫茜茸灑面作點綴。

* 饅頭切片。燒紅鑊將炸油煮沸，放入饅頭片炸至金黃色，撈起隔淨餘油。與魚翅湯一同食用。

Ingredients:

2 tbsp wine
8 cups water
6 slices ginger
6 shallots
1 lb (½ kg) frozen shark's fin
6 salted eggs
6 cups stock
1 tbsp corn oil
1 tbsp chopped ham
1 tsp chopped parsley
3 steamed buns
4 cups corn oil for deep frying

Seasoning-
1 tbsp wine
1 tsp salt
1 tsp light soy
½ tsp sugar
½ cube chicken essence
1/8 tsp pepper

Gravy Mix-
4 tbsp cornflour
⅓ cup water
½ tsp sesame oil

Method:

* *Heat the wok and sizzle the wine. Pour in 4 cups of the water, half the mashed ginger and shallots to bring to the boil. Simmer the shark's fin for 20 minutes. Drain and discard the ginger and shallots. Repeat the process once more.*

* *Boil the salted eggs for 3 minutes then place under a running tap to rinse till cool. Shell and keep the egg white for other dishes. Put the 6 egg yolks into a blender to mix with 1 cup of the stock till smooth.*

* *Heat the saucepan to bring the oil to boil. Sizzle the wine and pour in the remaining 5 cups of stock. Add the shark's fin to simmer for 30 minutes. Stir in the egg yolk mix and the seasoning then simmer for a further 10 minutes. Blend in the gravy mix to thicken. Sprinkle the ham and parsley on top to garnish.*

* *Slice the steamed buns. Heat the wok and bring the oil to boil. Deep fry the buns till light brown and drain. Serve hot with the shark's fin.*

柳暗花明
Shredded Beef with Bean Sprouts

材料：

牛柳6安（168克）
凍油3杯作泡油用
銀芽½磅（224克）
紅椒2隻
莥王或葱½安（14克）
葱頭2粒
蒜頭2粒
油4湯匙

醃肉料—生抽2茶匙
糖1茶匙
酒1茶匙
胡椒粉少許
生粉1茶匙
水⅓杯
油2湯匙（後下）

調味－酒 1 茶匙
　　　上湯 ¼ 杯
　　　蠔油 1 茶匙
　　　生抽 1 茶匙
　　　糖 ½ 茶匙
　　　胡椒粉少許

饙料－生粉 1 茶匙
　　　水 1 湯匙
　　　蔴油 1 茶匙

製法：

* 牛柳依橫紋切片，再切粗絲。加入醃料中醃 1 小時，再拌入油續醃30分鐘。
* 燒紅鑊，倒入凍油，隨即滑入牛柳泡油至半熟才撈起隔去餘油。將油傾回油桶內別用。
* 銀芽洗淨隔去水份。紅椒去籽切絲。
* 薑王洗淨切 1 吋（2.5公分）度。葱，蒜頭切片。
* 另鑊燒紅加油 2 湯匙煮沸，爆香葱蒜片各一半。倒下銀芽猛火炒 8 秒鐘，盛起候用。
* 再燒紅鑊加入餘油煮沸，爆香餘下葱蒜片。傾入牛柳絲，銀芽及紅椒絲迅速炒數下。潷酒加上湯再煮沸，倒入調味料及生粉水埋饙。最後灑薑王及蔴油上碟。

Ingredients:

6 oz (168 g) fillet steak
3 cups cool oil for parboiling
½ lb (224 g) bean sprouts
2 chillies
½ oz (14 g) white leeks or chives
2 shallots
2 garlic cloves
4 tbsp corn oil

Meat Marinade-
2 tsp light soy
1 tsp sugar
1 tsp wine
a pinch of pepper
1 tsp cornflour
⅓ cup water
2 tbsp corn oil, to be added last

Seasoning-
1 tsp sherry
¼ cup stock
1 tsp oyster sauce
1 tsp light soy
½ tsp sugar
a pinch of pepper

Gravy Mix-
1 tsp cornflour
1 tbsp water
1 tsp sesame oil

Method:

* *Shred and soak the beef with the marinade for an hour then blend in the oil to marinate for another 30 minutes.*
* *Heat the wok and pour in the cool oil. Immediately slide in the beef to parboil till half-cooked. Drain and pour the oil back into a container.*
* *Wash and drain the bean sprouts. Deseed and shred the chillies.*
* *Wash and cut the leeks into 1 inch section. Slice the shallots and garlic.*
* *Heat 2 tbsp of the oil in the wok to sauté half the shallots and garlic till fragrant. Stir fry the bean sprouts over high heat for about 8 seconds then remove.*
* *Reheat the wok to bring the remaining oil to boil. Sauté the remaining shallot and garlic. Pour in the beef, bean sprouts and chillies to stir fry briskly. Sizzle the wine, add the stock and pour in the mixed seasoning and the gravy mix. Garnish with the leeks and brighten the dish with the sesame oil. Dish and serve hot.*

遊龍戲鳳
Shredded Ham in Chicken Wings

材料：

酒1湯匙
水3杯
羌2片
鷄翼20隻
紅蘿蔔絲或西芹絲20條
火腿絲20條

油3湯匙
荠遠½磅（224克）
沸水1杯
鹽1茶匙
火腿茸1湯匙

調味－酒 1 茶匙
　　　上湯 ½ 杯
　　　鹽 ½ 茶匙
　　　糖 1 茶匙
　　　生抽 1 茶匙
　　　胡椒粉少許
　　　蔴油 ½ 茶匙

饋料－生粉 1 茶匙
　　　水 1 湯匙
　　　老抽 ¼ 茶匙
　　　蔴油 1 茶匙

製法：

* 燒紅鑊，潽酒加入水及羌片煮沸。
將雞翼放入飛水 5 至 6 分鐘，撈起
置水喉下冲淨脂肪，取出隔乾水份
後斬去頭尾 2 度，只餘中段。

* 將中段雞翼內之兩條骨取出，釀入
紅蘿蔔絲及火腿絲，排放在碟上。

* 再燒紅鑊加入油 1 湯匙煮沸，潽酒
½ 茶匙加上湯及調味料重煮沸，淋
在釀妥之雞翼上。放入蒸籠內蒸10
分鐘後取出，蒸雞上湯留起候用。

* 菜蓮放於沸水中加餘油及鹽 1 茶匙
飛水，撈起隔去水份，圍放在碟邊。

* 另鑊燒熱，潽下餘酒加蒸雞上湯。
調妥味後以生粉水埋饋，淋在雞翼
上，以火腿茸灑面上桌即成。

Ingredients:

1 tbsp wine
3 cups water
2 slices ginger
20 chicken wings
20 shredded carrots or celery
20 shredded Virginia ham
3 tbsp corn oil
½ lb (224 g) green vegetables
1 cup boiling water
1 tsp salt
1 tbsp chopped ham

Seasoning-
1 tsp wine
½ cup stock
½ tsp salt
1 tsp sugar
1 tsp light soy
a pinch of pepper
½ tsp sesame oil

Gravy Mix-
1 tsp cornflour
1 tbsp water
¼ tsp dark soy
1 tsp sesame oil

Method:

* *Heat the wok, sizzle the wine and pour in the water with the ginger to bring to the boil. Add the chicken wings to blanch for 5 to 6 minutes. Refresh under a running tap and drain. Cut away both ends of the wings and retain the middle section.*

* *Remove the bones from the wings and fill each hole with a piece of ham and carrot. Arrange on to a platter.*

* *Reheat the wok and bring 1 tbsp of the oil to boil. Sprinkle in half of the wine and add the stock and seasoning. Pour over the wings and steam for 10 minutes. Remove and retain the stock for later use.*

* *Blanch the vegetables in the boiling water with the remaining oil and the salt. Remove and drain. Arrange along the edge of the platter.*

* *Heat another wok, sizzle the remaining wine and pour in the stock from the steamed chicken. Season to taste. Thicken the sauce with the gravy mix. Scoop on to the chicken wings then scatter the chopped ham on top and serve.*

春田大地
Shrimp Toasts with Quail's Eggs

材料：

鵪蛋16隻
水 3 杯
蝦20安（560克）
肥肉 2 安（56克）
沸水 1 杯
羌茸 ½ 茶匙
葱粒 1 茶匙
蛋白 1 隻
方飽 8 片
生粉 2 湯匙
火腿茸 2 茶匙
芫茜茸 2 茶匙
炸油 3 杯

調味料－鹽 ⅔ 茶匙
　　　　胡椒粉 ¼ 茶匙
　　　　鷄粉 ¼ 茶匙
　　　　蔴油 1 茶匙
　　　　生粉 2 茶匙

製法：

* 鵪蛋放入水中焓 5 分鐘，取出沖凍
  去殼。
* 蝦去殼挑腸，洗淨抹乾壓爛成茸，
  轉放入深碗內。
* 肥肉放於沸水中飛水，撈起沖凍隔
  去水份。剁幼與羌茸、葱粒、蛋白
  及調味料一同放入蝦泥中。以手搓
  至起膠。置雪柜內雪 1 小時。
* 方飽去邊切成兩塊長方八角形。每
  塊方飽灑上少許生粉。將蝦膠堆放
  在上面，中間放上一隻鵪蛋。兩邊
  分放火腿茸與芫茜茸，以手按緊。
* 燒紅鑊加油煮沸，將蝦膠滑入鑊中
  炸至兩面金黃色。以罩籬撈起隔去
  餘油，排放在碟中即可上桌。

Ingredients:

16 quails' eggs
3 cups water
20 oz (560 g) shrimps
2 oz (56 g) fat pork
1 cup boiling water
½ tsp minced ginger
1 tsp chopped spring onions
1 egg white
8 pieces of bread
2 tbsp cornflour
2 tsp minced ham
2 tsp chopped parsley
3 cups corn oil for deep frying

Seasoning-
2/3 tsp salt
¼ tsp pepper
¼ tsp chicken powder
1 tsp sesame oil
2 tsp cornflour

Method:

* *Boil the quails' eggs in the water for 5 minutes then refresh and shell.*
* *Shell and devein the shrimps. Wash, dry and mash into a purée then place in a deep mixing bowl.*
* *Blanch the fat pork in the boiling water, refresh and drain. Mince and add into the shrimp puree together with the minced ginger, spring onions, egg white and the seasoning to pound until elastic. Leave in the refrigerator to chill for an hour.*
* *Cut the edges of the bread and halve into rectangular slices. Dust the bread with the cornflour. Heap the shrimp purée on each piece of bread then place a quails' egg in the centre. Sprinkle the chopped ham and parsley at both ends.*
* *Heat the wok and bring the oil to the boil. Slide in the shrimps toast to deep fry until both sides are golden brown. Drain and serve hot.*

壽比南山
Spicy Chicken in Pumpkin

材料：

南瓜1個約重4磅（2公斤）
童雞2磅（1公斤）
羌2片
葱2棵
五香炒米粉2安（56克）
油4杯作泡油用

調味料一鹽 $\frac{1}{2}$ 茶匙
　　　　糖2湯匙
　　　　雞粉 $\frac{1}{4}$ 茶匙
　　　　紹酒1湯匙
　　　　南乳1湯匙
　　　　老抽 $\frac{1}{2}$ 湯匙

製法：

* 南瓜依皮上凹凸紋切開頂部使成蓋子（看圖）。將瓜子全部挖去，瓜身當作燉盅。
* 雞洗擦乾淨以毛巾吸乾水份，斬成大件候用。
* 羌片及葱剁茸，與上述調味料及五香米粉撈勻，將雞件放入醃20分鐘。
* 燒紅鑊加入油煮至微溫時，即將雞件放入泡油2分鐘。取出隔淨餘油。
* 將隔淨油之雞件轉盛在南瓜內，蓋上瓜蓋。放入蒸籠內蒸40分鐘。取出上桌，甘香濃郁，可酒可飯。

Ingredients:

1 pumpkin, about 4 lb (2 kg)
2 lb (1 kg) spring chicken
2 slices ginger
2 spring onions
2 oz (56 g) spicy rice flour
4 cups oil for parboiling

Seasoning-
½ tsp salt
2 tbsp sugar
¼ tsp chicken powder
1 tbsp yellow wine
1 tbsp fermented red beancurd
½ tbsp dark soy

Method:

* *Cut and carve the pumpkin to form a pot with a lid. (Refer to photograph). Remove all the seeds.*
* *Wash, clean and dry the chicken. Chop into serving pieces.*
* *Mince the ginger and spring onions to mix well with the seasoning and rice flour. Put the chicken in to the mixed seasoning to marinate for 20 minutes.*
* *Heat the wok and add the oil to heat until warm. Pour in the chicken to parboil for 2 minutes. Remove and drain.*
* *Transfer the chicken in to the pumpkin and cover with the lid. Place in the steamer and cook over high heat for 40 minutes. Remove on to a platter and serve hot.*

老少平安
Steamed Bean Curd with Fish Paste

材料：

板豆腐1磅（½公斤）
蝦肉4安（112克）
魚柳4安（112克）
蛋白1隻
羗茸1湯匙
葱粒2湯匙
生粉1湯匙
摘妥芫茜1茶匙
熟油1茶匙
老抽1茶匙

調味料—鹽1茶匙
　　　　糖1茶匙
　　　　鷄粉¼茶匙
　　　　胡椒粉⅛茶匙
　　　　蔴油1茶匙
　　　　生粉2茶匙

製法：

* 豆腐洗淨隔去水份放入深盆中搞爛
  成茸候用。
* 蝦肉挑腸洗淨，用毛巾抹乾後壓爛
  成茸。留起數隻作爲裝飾用。
* 魚柳洗淨抹乾後切片剁爛成茸。將
  蝦茸及魚茸混合物一同放入深碗中
  ，加調味料及蛋白撈勻後用手撻至
  起膠。羗、葱茸加入再撻至均勻。
* 蝦，魚茸加入豆腐中搞勻，將生粉
  拌入再搞片刻。
* 碟中塗油少許，將混合物倒入抹平
  ，上放蝦肉數隻點綴。置蒸籠內蒸
  10分鐘，取出灑芫茜加熟油、老抽
  在上即成。

Ingredients:

1 lb (½ kg) soft bean curd
4 oz (112 g) shelled shrimps
4 oz (112 g) fish fillet
1 egg white
1 tbsp minced ginger
2 tbsp chopped spring onions
1 tbsp cornflour
1 tsp trimmed parsley
1 tsp cooked oil
1 tsp dark soy

Seasoning-
1 tsp salt
1 tsp sugar
¼ tsp chicken powder
1/8 tsp pepper
1 tsp sesame oil
2 tsp cornflour

Method:

* *Wash, drain and mash the beancurd in a deep bowl.*
* *Devein and wash the shrimps. Dry
  with a towel then mash into a
  purée or mince in a food processor. Leave a few shrimps for
  garnishing.*
* *Wash and dry the fish fillet. Slice
  and mince into a paste. Mix the
  shrimp and fish purée in a bowl
  with the seasoning and egg white
  and pound until firm. Stir in the
  ginger and chopped spring onions
  to mix thoroughly.*
* *Combine the fish and shrimp
  purée with the mashed beancurd.
  Put in the cornflour to stir until
  well-blended.*
* *Fill a greased platter with the
  mixture. Smoothen the surface
  and garnish with the whole
  shrimps. Place into a steamer and
  cook for 10 minutes. Remove and
  sprinkle the parsley, cooked oil
  and dark soy on top. Serve hot.*

一團和氣
Stewed Pork Shoulder

材料：

元蹄3磅（1½公斤）
粗鹽2湯匙
油2½湯匙
羗4片
葱頭4粒
水6杯
八角4粒

老抽1湯匙
炸油½鑊
大地魚1條
生菜1棵
沸水2杯
鹽1茶匙

調味料—紹酒 2 湯匙
　　　　鹽 ½ 茶匙
　　　　南乳 3 湯匙
　　　　生抽 1 茶匙
　　　　老抽 1 茶匙
　　　　糖 2 湯匙
　　　　鷄精 1 粒

製法：

* 將元蹄用粗鹽擦去皮上污垢，洗淨抹乾水份。
* 燒紅鑊加入 ½ 湯匙油，爆香一半羌片及葱頭。瀪酒 1 湯匙加水煮沸。將元蹄及八角 2 粒放入文火煮約 1 小時，取出隔乾水份，在豬皮上塗上老抽。
* 再燒紅鑊將炸油煮沸，放入元蹄炸至金紅色，取出置入水喉下洗淨。
* 大地魚洗淨放入以上炸油中炸脆，搗碎成茸。生菜洗淨候用。
* 深鍋一個燒熱加入油 1 湯匙，瀪下餘酒 1 湯匙傾入元蹄之原汁煮沸，再加入大地魚末，另一半羌、葱頭、八角及調味料。重將元蹄放入鍋內煮約 2 小時至皮酥肉爛爲止。
* 生菜放入沸水中加鹽及餘油飛水，撈起隔去水份排放在碟上。元蹄整隻放在生菜上，用利刀稍鋸數刀，將原汁淋在上面即成。

Ingredients:

3 lb (1½ kg) shoulder of pork
2 tbsp coarse salt
2½ tbsp oil
4 slices ginger
4 shallots
6 cups water
4 star anises
1 tbsp dark soy
½ wok corn oil for deep frying
1 dried plaice
1 lettuce
2 cups boiling water
1 tsp salt

Seasoning-
2 tbsp sherry
½ tsp salt
3 tbsp fermented red beancurd
1 tsp light soy
1 tsp dark soy
2 tbsp sugar
1 cube chicken essence

Method:

* *Rub the pig's skin with the salt then singe, clean and drain.*
* *Heat a wok with ½ tbsp of the oil to sauté half of the ginger and shallots. Sizzle in 1 tbsp of the sherry and add the water to bring to boil. Put in the pork and 2 star anises to simmer over low heat for 1 hour. Drain and coat the pork with the dark soy.*
* *Bring the oil to the boil in a wok to deep fry the pork until golden brown. Wash under a running tap.*
* *Clean the plaice and deep fry until crisp then mash into a powder. Wash the lettuce thoroughly.*
* *Heat a saucepan with 1 tbsp oil. Sizzle the remaining tbsp of sherry and pour in the pork sauce to bring to the boil. Add the plaice powder, the remaining ginger, shallots and star anises together with the seasoning. Return the pork into the saucepan and stew for 2 hours until soft and tender.*
* *Blanch the lettuce in the boiling water with the salt and the remaining tbsp of oil. Drain and arrange on to the platter. Place the whole piece of pork shoulder on the lettuce and cut into sections. Pour the sauce on top and serve.*

橫財順利
Stewed Tongue with Black Moss

材料：

豬脷2條，每條約8安（224克）
沸水4½杯
油5湯匙
羌4片
葱4棵
八角1湯匙
花椒½茶匙
髮菜1安（28克）
紅蘿蔔3安（84克）

調味料—酒1茶匙
上湯3杯
生抽1湯匙
蠔油1湯匙
糖1茶匙
鷄粉¼茶匙

餡料－生粉 1 茶匙
　　　水 1 湯匙
　　　老抽 ½ 茶匙
　　　蔴油 1 茶匙

製法：

* 豬脷放於 3 杯沸水中飛水 5 分鐘，
  取出過冷河隔乾水份，用小刀刮去
  脷苔及污漬。
* 燒紅鑊加油 2 湯匙，爆香一半羗片
  及葱，將豬脷加入爆炒。潲酒加上
  湯，八角及花椒煮沸以文火續煮 1
  小時。取出置一旁攤凍。豬脷汁留
  起候用。
* 髮菜浸透洗淨，放於另 1 杯沸水中
  飛水 30 秒鐘，撈起過冷河隔乾水份
  。沸水留作紅蘿蔔飛水用。
* 燒紅鑊加入油 2 湯匙爆香其餘羗及
  葱，倒入餘下 ½ 杯水煮沸。加入髮
  菜煮約 2 分鐘取出。
* 紅蘿蔔切花放於以上 1 杯沸水中飛
  水，撈起隔去水份。
* 豬脷切片圍放碟邊。紅蘿蔔片排在
  內圈。髮菜放在中央。
* 鑊洗淨再燒熱加入豬脷汁煮沸。試
  妥味以生粉水打餡，淋在豬脷及髮
  菜上即成。

Ingredients:

*2 pigs' tongues, about 8 oz (224 g)
  each
4½ cups boiling water
5 tbsp corn oil
4 slices ginger
4 spring onions
1 tbsp star anises
½ tsp xanthoxylum seeds
1 oz (28 g) black moss
3 oz (84 g) carrots*

*Seasoning-
1 tsp wine
3 cups stock
1 tbsp light soy
1 tbsp oyster sauce
1 tsp sugar
¼ tsp chicken powder*

*Gravy Mix-
1 tsp cornflour
1 tbsp water
½ tsp dark soy
1 tsp sesame oil*

Method:

* *Blanch the tongues in 3 cups of
  the boiling water for 5 minutes.
  Refresh and drain. Scrape with a
  small knife to remove the white
  skin.*
* *Heat the wok with 2 tbsp of the
  oil to sauté half of the ginger and
  spring onions to bring out the
  fragrance. Add the pig's tongue
  to fry well. Sizzle the wine and
  add the stock, the star anises and
  xanthoxylum seeds to bring to
  the boil. Simmer for 1 hour.
  Remove and leave aside to cool.
  Keep the juice for later use.*
* *Soak and clean the black moss.
  Blanch in another cup of the
  boiling water for 30 seconds then
  refresh and drain. Retain the
  water to blanch the carrots.*
* *Heat the wok with another 2 tbsp
  of oil to sauté the remaining
  ginger and spring onions. Pour in
  the remaining ½ cup of water to
  bring to boil. Add the black moss
  to simmer for 2 minutes.
  Remove.*
* *Carve the carrots and blanch in
  the above 1 cup of boiling water.
  Rinse and drain.*
* *Slice the tongues and arrange
  into a circle on a platter. Put the
  sliced carrots inside the circle
  with the moss in the centre.*
* *Clean and reheat the wok to
  bring the juice to the boil. Season
  to taste then blend in the gravy
  mix to thicken. Pour on to the
  pigs' tongue and black moss and
  serve immediately.*

橫財就手
Stewed Trotter with Black Moss

材料：

豬手1隻約2磅（1公斤）
沸水5杯
髮菜1安（28克）
羗汁1茶匙
酒1茶匙
生菜1磅（½公斤）
鹽1茶匙

鷄粉1茶匙
油4湯匙
羗2片
葱頭2粒
蒜頭2粒
八角2粒

調味－南乳 3 湯匙
　　　紹酒 1 湯匙
　　　上湯 2 杯
　　　鹽 ¼ 茶匙
　　　糖 2 湯匙

饎料－生粉 1 茶匙
　　　水 1 湯匙
　　　老抽 ½ 茶匙
　　　蔴油 1 湯匙

製法：

* 豬手斬開，骨離而皮相連，使成一整塊。用小刀刮淨再以火燒去細毛，放入 3 杯沸水中飛水片刻。取出洗淨隔乾水份。
* 髮菜洗淨浸透，放入另 1 杯沸水中加薑汁及酒飛水。撈起過冷河隔乾水份。
* 生菜洗淨，放入餘下沸水中加鹽，雞粉及油 2 湯匙焗約20秒鐘。撈起隔去水份排放在碟上。薑切絲。葱頭及蒜頭切片。
* 燒紅鑊加入餘油煮沸，爆香薑、葱、蒜。將南乳搗爛加入炒透。倒下豬手，潷酒再加上湯拌勻。轉放壓力保中加八角以文火煮25分鐘。
* 揭開保蓋，加入髮菜及調味料，再蓋上保蓋續煮 5 分鐘，盛在生菜碟上。餘汁以生粉水埋饎淋在上面即可上桌。

Ingredients:

1 pig's trotter, about 2 lb (1 kg)
5 cups boiling water
1 oz (28 g) black moss
1 tsp ginger juice
1 tsp wine
1 lb (½ kg) lettuce
1 tsp salt
1 tsp chicken powder
4 tbsp corn oil
2 slices ginger
2 shallots
2 garlic cloves
2 star anises

Seasoning-
3 tbsp fermented red bean curd
1 tbsp cooking sherry
2 cups stock
¼ tsp salt
2 tbsp sugar

Gravy Mix-
1 tsp cornflour
1 tbsp water
½ tsp dark soy
1 tsp sesame oil

Method:

* Slit along the centre of the trotter and cut it lengthwise, but do not slice through. Scrape and singe the skin. Blanch in 3 cups of the boiling water for a minute. Rinse and drain.
* Soak and clean the black moss. Blanch in another cup of the boiling water with the ginger juice and wine. Refresh and drain.
* Wash and blanch the lettuce in the remaining boiling water with the salt, chicken powder and 2 tbsp of the oil for 20 seconds. Drain and arrange on to a platter. Shred the ginger. Slice the shallots and garlic.
* Heat the wok to bring the remaining oil to the boil. Sauté the ginger, shallots and garlic till aromatic. Mash the red bean curd and pour into the wok to fry well. Add the trotter and sizzle the wine. Pour in the stock to stir thoroughly. Transfer into a pressure cooker and add the star anises to simmer for 25 minutes.
* Remove the lid and add the black moss and seasoning. Cover to simmer for another 5 minutes. Move on to the bed of lettuce. Thicken the sauce with the gravy mix then pour over the trotter and lettuce to serve.

東成西就

Stewed Trotter with Mushrooms

材料：

豬手1隻約1磅（½公斤）　　　糖1菜匙
沸水6杯　　　　　　　　　　油4湯匙
羌2片　　　　　　　　　　　髮菜½安（14克）
葱頭2粒　　　　　　　　　　蒜頭1粒
紅蘿蔔3安（84克）　　　　　南乳3湯匙
生菜8安（224克）　　　　　熟冬菇4安（112克）
鹽1湯匙

調味－酒 2 茶匙
　　　水 3 至 4 杯
　　　鹽 ⅟₄ 茶匙
　　　糖 2 湯匙
　　　胡椒粉少許
　　　蔴油 ⅟₂ 茶匙

製法：

* 豬手以小刀刮淨，再用火燒去細毛，洗淨後斬件。置 3 杯沸水中加羌 1 片及葱頭 1 粒煮20分鐘。取出用凍水冲洗乾淨。
* 紅蘿蔔切片。生菜洗淨一同放入 2 杯沸水中加鹽，糖及油 1 湯匙飛水。撈起隔乾排放碟上。
* 髮菜浸透洗淨放入餘下沸水中飛水，撈起置水喉下冲凍隔乾。將餘下羌片，葱頭及蒜頭切絲。
* 燒紅鑊加油 2 湯匙煮沸爆香羌、葱、蒜。加入南乳及豬手爆透。潅酒加水蓋過豬手，猛火煮10分鐘，轉置壓力煲內炆15分鐘。
* 鑊再燒紅加入餘油煮沸爆香冬菇，將豬手重放回鑊中煮10分鐘，加入髮菜續煮 5 分鐘。調妥味將冬菇、豬手及髮菜倒在菜上。以紅蘿蔔片點綴上桌。

Ingredients:

1 pig's trotter, about 1 lb (½ kg)
6 cups boiling water
2 slices ginger
2 shallots
3 oz (84 g) carrots
8 oz (224 g) lettuce
1 tbsp salt
1 tsp sugar
4 tbsp corn oil
½ oz (14 g) black moss
1 garlic clove
3 tbsp fermented bean curd
4 oz (112 g) cooked Chinese mushrooms

Seasoning-
2 tsp wine
3 to 4 cups water
¼ tsp salt
2 tbsp sugar
a pinch of pepper
½ tsp sesame oil

Method:

* *Scrape, singe and chop the trotter, then place in 3 cups of the boiling water with a piece of ginger and 1 shallot to cook for 20 minutes. Refresh and drain.*
* *Slice the carrots and wash the lettuce. Blanch them in 2 cups of the boiling water with the salt, sugar and 1 tbsp of the oil. Drain and dish on a platter.*
* *Soak, clean and blanch the black moss in the remaining cup of boiling water. Rinse under a running tap and drain. Shred the other slice of ginger, shallot and the garlic.*
* *Heat the wok with 2 tbsp of the oil. Sauté the ginger, shallot and garlic till aromatic. Add the fermented bean curd and trotter to fry well. Sizzle the wine, pour in the water to cover the trotter and bring to boil over high heat. Stew for 10 minutes then transfer into a pressure cooker and continue stewing for another 15 minutes. Alternatively, transfer into a saucepan and stew for another hour. Remove.*
* *Heat the remaining oil in the wok to sauté the mushrooms and return the trotter into the wok to boil for 10 minutes. Add the black moss to cook for another 5 minutes. Season to taste. Arrange the mushrooms, trotter and black moss on a bed of lettuce. Garnish with the carrot slices and serve.*

錦上添花
Stuffed Bean Curd with Vegetables

材料：

實豆腐8件
魚肉6安（168克）
馬蹄2粒
葱粒1湯匙
生粉2湯匙
油4湯匙
蒜頭1片
葱絲2湯匙 裝飾
菜薳½磅（224克）

沸水2杯
鹽1茶匙

醃魚料－鹽1茶匙
　　　　糖½茶匙
　　　　胡椒粉少許
　　　　生粉1茶匙
　　　　蔴油½茶匙

調味料－酒 1 茶匙
　　　　上湯 ½ 杯
　　　　蠔油 1 茶匙
　　　　胡椒粉少許

饎料 —— 生粉 ½ 茶匙
　　　　水 1 湯匙
　　　　蔴油 1 茶匙

製法：

* 豆腐每件對角切爲三角件，以刀鏎
  開中央挖去豆腐少許。
* 魚肉洗淨抹乾放入大碗中剁爛成茸
  。
* 馬蹄去皮洗淨切粒，與葱粒及調味
  料一同放入魚茸中搞勻，用手搓至
  起膠。
* 豆腐之開口處塗上少許生粉，將魚
  茸釀入。
* 燒紅鏎加入油 2 湯匙煮沸，將釀好
  之豆腐放入先煎有肉之一邊。後煎
  其他各邊至微黃色，即可盛起隔淨
  餘油。
* 再燒紅鏎加油 1 湯匙爆香蒜片。讚
  酒加上湯煮沸，將釀豆腐重放鏎中
  煮 3 分鐘。試妥味後以生粉水埋饎
  ，灑上蔴油即可上碟。
* 菜薳洗淨放於沸水中加入餘油 1 湯
  匙及鹽飛水。撈起隔去水份圍在釀
  豆腐旁邊即可上桌。

Ingredients:

8 pieces solid bean curd
6 oz (168 g) fish fillet
2 water chestnuts
1 tbsp chopped spring onions
2 tbsp cornflour
4 tbsp corn oil
1 sliced garlic
2 tbsp shredded spring onions for
  garnishing
½ lb (224 g) green vegetables
2 cups boiling water
1 tsp salt.

Fish Marinade-
¼ tsp salt
½ tsp sugar
a pinch of pepper
1 tsp cornflour
½ tsp sesame oil

Seasoning-
1 tsp wine
½ cup stock
1 tsp oyster sauce
a pinch of pepper

Gravy Mix-
½ tsp cornflour
1 tbsp water
1 tsp sesame oil

Method:

* Cut each piece of the beancurd
  into two triangles. Slit the centre
  with a small knife and scoop out
  a little of the bean curd.
* Wash, dry and mince the fish
  then place into a mixing bowl.
* Peel, wash and dice the water
  chestnuts then add into the fish
  purée with the chopped spring
  onions and the seasoning. Pound
  until elastic.
* Dust each slit of the beancurd
  with the cornflour and stuff in
  the fish purée.
* Heat the wok to bring 2 tbsp of
  the oil to boil. Slide in the stuffed
  beancurds with the fish side
  facing down. Shallow fry till all
  sides are golden brown. Remove
  and drain.
* Reheat the wok and add another
  tbsp of the oil to sauté the sliced
  garlic. Sizzle the wine and pour
  in the stock to bring to boil.
  Return the beancurd into the
  wok and season to taste. Simmer
  for 3 minutes. Stir in the gravy
  mix to thicken the sauce. Sprinkle
  in the sesame oil and dish.
* Wash and blanch the vegetables
  in the boiling water with the
  remaining tbsp of oil and salt.
  Drain and arrange round the
  stuffed bean curds and serve hot.

百年好合

Stuffed Mushrooms in Batter

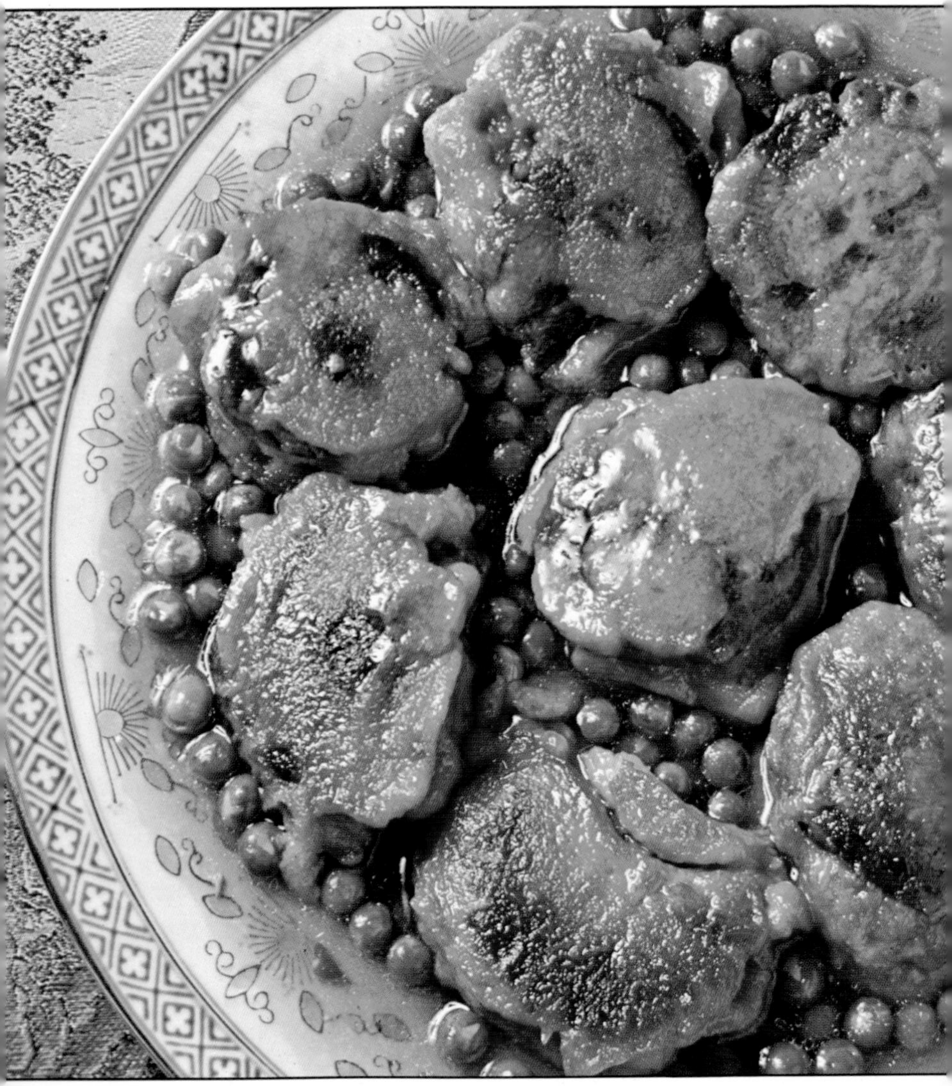

材料：

大冬菇24隻
豬肉$\frac{1}{2}$磅（224克）
馬蹄6粒
葱2棵
青豆$\frac{1}{2}$杯
沸水1杯
生粉2湯匙
麵粉$\frac{1}{2}$杯
水$\frac{1}{4}$杯
油2湯匙

醃冬菇料－鹽$\frac{1}{4}$茶匙
糖$\frac{1}{2}$茶匙
油1湯匙

醃肉料──酒1茶匙
生抽1湯匙
糖1茶匙
生粉$\frac{1}{2}$湯匙
蛋$\frac{1}{2}$隻
胡椒粉少許

調味料－酒1茶匙
上湯$\frac{1}{2}$杯
生抽$\frac{1}{2}$湯匙
糖$\frac{1}{2}$茶匙
鷄粉$\frac{1}{8}$茶匙
蔴油1茶匙

製法：

* 冬菇洗淨浸至軟，揸出水份後剪去蒂，加入醃冬菇料中撈勻，置蒸籠內蒸10分鐘。
* 豬肉洗淨剁爛。馬蹄去皮切粒。葱摘妥切粒。將豬肉茸放在大碗內，加入醃肉料搞勻，再倒入馬蹄粒及葱粒拌勻用手撻至起膠，轉放入雪柜中雪30分鐘。
* 青豆放於沸水中飛水，冲淨隔去水份候用。
* 將12隻冬菇反轉放在桌上，每隻灑上少許生粉。肉餡分爲12份。將每隻冬菇釀上一份餡料，再把其餘12隻冬菇蓋在肉餡上，使成三文治形。
* 麵粉篩在碗中，加水和成稀麵糊。將每隻冬菇放入糊中拖勻。
* 燒紅鑊加油煮沸，把上妥糊之冬菇滑入鑊中煎至兩面金黃色。濳酒加上湯及調味料，以文火炆至汁差不多乾時，加入青豆及蔴油。即可上碟。

Ingredients:

24 dried Chinese mushrooms
½ lb (224 g) pork
6 water chestnuts
2 spring onions
½ cup sweet peas
1 cup boiling water
2 tbsp cornflour
½ cup flour
¼ cup water
2 tbsp corn oil

Mushroom Marinade-
¼ tsp salt
½ tsp sugar
1 tbsp corn oil

Pork Marinade-
1 tsp wine
1 tbsp light soy
1 tsp sugar
½ tbsp cornflour
½ egg
a pinch of pepper

Seasoning-
1 tsp wine
½ cup stock
½ tbsp light soy
½ tsp sugar
1/8 tsp M.S.G
1 tsp sesame oil

Method:

* *Clean and soak the mushrooms until softened. Squeeze out the excess water; cut off the stalks and mix well with the marinade then steam for 10 minutes.*
* *Clean and mince the pork. Peel and dice the water chestnuts finely. Trim and chop the spring onions. Place the minced pork in a mixing bowl and drop in the marinade to pound well. Stir in the water chestnuts and spring onions and continue pounding until elastic. Leave in the refrigerator to chill for 30 minutes.*
* *Blanch the peas in the boiling water then refresh and drain.*
* *Dust the inside of each mushroom with some cornflour. Divide the meat filling into 12 portions then sandwich each portion between 2 mushrooms, making a total of 12 pairs.*
* *Sift the flour into a bowl and blend into a thin batter with the water. Dip the stuffed mushrooms in the batter to coat evenly.*
* *Heat the wok to bring the oil to boil. Arrange the stuffed mushrooms to shallow fry until both sides are golden brown. Sizzle the wine, add the stock and seasoning. Simmer over low heat until the liquid is nearly dried. Slide in the peas and sprinkle in the sesame oil. Remove and dish.*

堆金砌玉
Stuffed Peppers with Golden Corn

材料：

細燈籠椒½磅（224克）
生粉3湯匙
蝦肉1磅（½公斤）
粗鹽1湯匙
肥肉2安（56克）（隨意）
沸水2杯
葱粒1湯匙
紅椒2隻
粟米10安（280克）

紅蘿蔔粒¼杯
油6湯匙
葱頭1粒切片

醃料－鹽½茶匙
　　　糖¼茶匙
　　　胡椒粉少許
　　　生粉2茶匙
　　　蔴油½茶匙

調味－鹽¼茶匙
　　　酒1茶匙
　　　上湯¾杯
　　　生抽1茶匙
　　　糖1茶匙

饋料－生粉2茶匙
　　　水2湯匙
　　　蔴油1茶匙

製法：

* 燈籠椒洗淨切去頂部，去籽後在內邊拍上薄薄一層生粉，放置一旁候用。
* 蝦肉挑去腸臟，以粗鹽撈勻，置水喉下洗淨用毛巾抹乾水份，排放在砧板上以刀壓爛成茸，轉放深碗中候用。
* 肥肉放於 1 杯沸水中焓熟，撈起沖凍隔去水份切幼粒。
* 醃料拌勻放入蝦茸中搞勻略撻。隨即加入肥肉粒及葱粒續撻至起膠。放入雪柜內雪 1 小時。
* 紅椒去籽切粒。粟米及紅蘿蔔粒放入餘下沸水中飛水，取出沖凍隔乾水份。
* 燒紅鑊加油 1 湯匙煮沸，灑鹽爆香葱頭片。倒入紅椒粒及紅蘿蔔粒拌炒，加入粟米兜勻盛在碟上。
* 將蝦膠釀入每隻辣椒內。
* 再燒紅鑊加入油 3 湯匙煮沸，將釀妥之燈籠椒放入鑊中以文火煎至金黃色，取出排放在粟米粒上。
* 鑊洗淨再燒熱加入餘油，潷酒加上湯及調味，以生粉水慢慢流入和成饡。滴入蔴油淋在釀辣椒上即可上桌。

Ingredients:

½ lb (224 g) small bell capsicums
3 tbsp cornflour
1 lb (½ kg) shelled shrimps
1 tbsp coarse salt
2 oz (56 g) fat pork (optional)
2 cups boiling water
1 tbsp chopped spring onions
2 chillies
10 oz (280 g) sweet corn
¼ cup diced carrots
6 tbsp corn oil
1 sliced shallot

Marinade-	Seasoning-
½ tsp salt	¼ tsp salt
¼ tsp sugar	1 tsp wine
a pinch of pepper	¾ cup stock
2 tsp cornflour	1 tsp light soy
½ tsp sesame oil	1 tsp sugar

Gravy Mix-
2 tsp cornflour
2 tbsp water
1 tsp sesame oil

Method:

* *Wash and cut off the top of the capsicums. Deseed and dust the inside with the cornflour then leave aside for later use.*
* *Devein and toss the shrimps with the coarse salt. Wash and dry with a towel then mince into a purée in a food processor. Remove and place into a mixing bowl.*
* *Cook the fat pork in 1 cup of the boiling water. Rinse, dry and dice finely.*
* *Stir the mixed marinade into the shrimp purée and pound well. Add the fat pork and the chopped spring onions and continue pounding until elastic. Chill in the refrigerator for an hour.*
* *Deseed and dice the chillies. Blanch the sweet corn and the carrots in the remaining boiling water, refresh and drain.*
* *Heat the wok with 1 tbsp of the oil and sprinkle in the salt then sauté the shallot. Pour in the chillies and carrots to stir well. Add the sweet corn to mix thoroughly and dish.*
* *Stuff the capsicums with the shrimp purée.*
* *Reheat the wok and bring the other 3 tbsp of oil to boil. Place the stuffed capsicums in the wok to shallow fry over low heat until cooked and golden. Remove and arrange on the bed of sweet corn.*
* *Clean and heat the wok again with the remaining oil. Sizzle the wine, add the stock and seasoning to bring to the boil. Stream the cornflour mix into the stock to thicken. Drop in the sesame oil and pour over the stuffed capsicums then serve hot.*

黃金滿掌
Stuffed Webs with Mashed Shrimps

材料：

蝦肉1磅（½公斤）	芫茜2棵	醃蝦料—生粉1茶匙
粗鹽2湯匙	鷄粉1湯匙	鹽½茶匙
肥肉2安（56克）	生粉2湯匙	胡椒粉少許
沸水8杯	油2湯匙	蛋白½隻
鴨掌24隻	蛋白2隻	
羌茸1安（28克）		調味——酒1茶匙　　糖¾茶匙
葱茸1安（28克）		上湯¾杯　　胡椒粉¼茶匙
酒2湯匙		鹽¼茶匙
鹹蛋王3隻		

饀料－生粉 1 茶匙
　　　水 1 湯匙

製法：

* 蝦挑腸後放在筲箕內加鹽 1 湯匙拋勻。置水喉下冲洗乾淨，放在乾毛巾上吸乾水份，轉置砧板上以刀拍爛成茸。
* 肥肉放於½杯沸水中飛水至透明，取出洗淨切幼粒。加入蝦茸內再將醃料拌入，以手搓至起膠。
* 鴨掌以餘下之鹽擦淨洗妥，放於另 6 杯沸水中加羌，葱茸及酒各半煮 25 分鐘，撈起以清水浸凍，拆去骨頭。鹹蛋王切粒。芫茜洗淨摘妥。
* 將餘下 1½杯沸水傾下鑊中，加入餘下之羌葱茸，酒及雞粉煮沸。倒入去骨鴨掌煮 5 分鐘。撈起過冷河隔乾水份。
* 鴨掌內塗生粉少許，將蝦膠釀入掌內，在最高處按一凹位放入鹹蛋王一粒，全部排放碟上蒸 5 分鐘。
* 燒紅鑊加油煮沸，潷酒加上湯及調味料，以生粉水埋饀。沸時加入蛋白拌勻淋在鴨掌上。以芫茜點綴上桌。

Ingredients:

1 lb (½ kg) shelled shrimps
2 tbsp coarse salt
2 oz (56 g) fat pork
8 cups boiling water
24 ducks' webs
1 oz (28 g) mashed ginger
1 oz (28 g) mashed spring onions
2 tbsp wine
3 salted egg yolks
2 parsley sprigs
1 tbsp chicken powder
2 tbsp cornflour
2 tbsp corn oil
2 egg whites

Shrimp Marinade-
1 tsp cornflour
½ tsp salt
a pinch of pepper
½ egg white

Seasoning-
1 tsp cooking sherry
¾ cup stock
¼ tsp salt
¾ tsp sugar
¼ tsp pepper

Gravy Mix-
1 tsp cornflour
1 tbsp water

Method:

* Devein the shrimps then sprinkle in 1 tbsp of the coarse salt to toss well. Wash under a running tap and dry with a towel. Mash the shrimps into a purée.
* Blanch the fat pork with ½ cup of the boiling water until transparent. Refresh and dice finely. Stir into the shrimp purée then blend in the mixed marinade. Pound until firm and elastic.
* Rub the webs with the remaining coarse salt and wash thoroughly. Blanch in another 6 cups of the boiling water with half of the ginger, spring onions and wine. Simmer for 25 minutes then refresh and debone. Dice the salted egg yolks. Trim and wash the parsley.
* Place the remaining 1½ cups of boiling water in the wok, add the remaining ginger, spring onions, wine and the chicken powder to bring to the boil. Put in the webs to simmer for 5 minutes. Remove, refresh and drain.
* Dry and coat the inside of the webs with the cornflour. Stuff in the shrimp purée and top with the diced egg yolk. Steam for 5 minutes.
* Heat the wok to bring the oil to the boil. Sizzle the wine, add the stock and seasoning. Thicken the stock with the gravy mix then stir in the egg white after the gravy has been boiled. Mask on to the stuffed webs. Garnish with the parsley.

綽有餘裕
Sweet and Sour Fish

材料：

鯉魚 1 條 1½ 磅（¾ 公斤）
胡椒粉少許
青椒 1 隻
紅蘿蔔 2 安（56克）
笋 2 安（56克）（隨意）
沸水 1 杯
熟冬菇 2 隻
葱 2 棵
芫茜 2 棵
油 3 湯匙
羗茸 1 茶匙
葱頭 1 粒切片

調味—酒 1 湯匙
　　　上湯 1 杯
　　　鹽 ½ 茶匙
　　　生抽 1 湯匙
　　　老抽 ½ 湯匙
　　　糖 2 湯匙
　　　鷄粉 ¼ 茶匙
　　　浙醋 2 湯匙

饋料—生粉 2 茶匙
　　　水 2 湯匙

製法：

* 鯉魚在頭部先拍一下將魚拍暈。打
  鱗開肚去腸臟洗淨抹乾。用刀在魚
  身兩邊各打橫鎅幾刀，每刀約相隔
  1吋。灑下胡椒粉塗勻，放入蒸籠
  內猛火蒸10分鐘。取出轉放在長碟
  上。
* 青椒去籽切絲。紅蘿蔔及笋一同放
  入沸水中飛水，撈起冲凍隔乾水份
  後切絲。
* 冬菇及葱切絲。芫茜洗淨摘妥。
* 燒紅鑊加油 2 湯匙爆香羗茸及葱頭
  片。濺酒倒入上湯煮沸，再加入雜
  菜絲及調味料兜勻。試妥味後以生
  粉水埋饋。將餘下 1 湯匙油拌入和
  勻，隨即淋在蒸熟之鯉魚上。最後
  灑下芫茜及葱絲即可上桌熱食。

Ingredients:

1 carp, about 1½ lb (¾ kg)
a pinch of pepper
1 capsicum
2 oz (56 g) carrots
2 oz (56 g) bamboo shoots (optional)
1 cup boiling water
2 cooked Chinese mushrooms
2 spring onions
2 parsley sprigs
3 tbsp corn oil
1 tsp minced ginger
1 sliced shallot

Seasoning-	Gravy Mix-
1 tbsp wine	*2 tsp cornflour*
1 cup stock	*2 tbsp water*
½ tsp salt	
1 tbsp light soy	
½ tbsp dark soy	
2 tbsp sugar	
¼ tsp chicken powder	
2 tbsp red vinegar	

Method:

* *Pat the head of carp with a chopper. Scale, gut, wash and dry. Crimp at intervals of 1" with a sharp knife on both sides. Sprinkle in the pepper evenly. Steam over high heat for 10 minutes. Remove and transfer on an oval platter.*
* *Deseed and shred the capsicum. Blanch the carrots and bamboo shoots in the boiling water. Refresh, drain and shred.*
* *Shred the mushrooms and spring onions. Clean and trim the parsley.*
* *Heat the wok with 2 tbsp of the oil to sauté the ginger and shallot. Sizzle the wine then pour in the stock. Add the shredded vegetables and season to taste. Thicken the stock with the gravy mix. Stir in the remaining tbsp of oil then pour on to the carp. Garnish with the parsley and shredded spring onions then serve hot.*

鵬程萬里
Sweet and Sour Fish Rolls

材料：

鯉魚1條約重2磅（1公斤）
熟冬菇4隻
笋或紅蘿蔔4安（112克）
沸水1杯
火腿2安（56克）
羗3片
葱3棵
生粉¼杯
炸油½鑊

油2湯匙
靑瓜1條作裝飾

醃魚料－羗汁1茶匙
　　　　生抽1茶匙
　　　　糖¼茶匙
　　　　胡椒粉少許
　　　　生粉1茶匙

脆漿－麵粉1杯
　　　發粉1茶匙
　　　鹽¼茶匙
　　　胡椒粉少許
　　　蛋白1隻
　　　水½杯
　　　油2湯匙

調味－酒１茶匙　　饋料－生粉２茶匙
　　　甜酸醋１杯　　　水２湯匙
　　　糖１茶匙　　　　胡椒粉少許
　　　　　　　　　　蔴油１茶匙

製法：

* 鯉魚去腸臟及皮，骨。起肉。片成大薄片。浸於醃料中醃15分鐘。

* 魚頭內邊從中切一刀拍扁，與魚尾一起放在塗油碟上，置蒸籠內猛火蒸６分鐘。

* 冬菇切絲。笋放入沸水中飛水，撈起冲凍隔乾水份切絲。火腿亦切絲。

* 羗，葱剁茸候用。

* 將每片魚肉放在桌上，三絲放在一邊捲起，以少許麵粉封口。

* 麵粉、發粉、鹽及胡椒粉一同放入碗中，加入蛋白及水搞勻成滑麵漿，再拌入油及蔴油撈勻。將魚卷放入沾滿粉漿。隨即放入炸油中炸至微黃，撈起隔去餘油，排放在長碟中央，魚頭尾分別擺放兩邊。

* 鑊燒紅加油煮沸爆香羗、葱茸，灒酒加甜酸醋煮沸。試妥味後以生粉水埋饋，灒下蔴油和勻淋在魚卷上。再以青瓜片圍在碟旁點綴。

Ingredients:

1 carp, about 2 lb (1 kg)
4 cooked Chinese mushrooms
4 oz (112 g) bamboo shoots or carrots
1 cup boiling water
2 oz (56 g) ham
3 slices ginger
3 spring onions
¼ cup cornflour
½ wok oil for deep frying
2 tbsp corn oil
1 cucumber for garnishing

Fish Marinade-
1 tsp ginger juice
1 tsp light soy
¼ tsp sugar
a pinch of pepper
1 tsp cornflour

Batter-
1 cup plain flour   *1 egg white*
1 tsp baking powder   *½ cup water*
¼ tsp salt   *2 tbsp corn oil*
a pinch of pepper

Seasoning-   *Gravy Mix-*
1 tsp wine   *2 tsp cornflour*
1 cup sweet sour sauce   *2 tbsp water*
1 tsp sugar   *pinch of pepper*
  1 tsp sesame oil

Method:

* *Gut, skin and debone the fish. Slice into big thin pieces and immerse in the marinade and leave for 15 minutes.*

* *Slit the head in the centre from the inside, open up and flatten slightly. Place on to a greased platter with the fish tail. Steam for 6 minutes over high heat.*

* *Shred the mushrooms. Blanch the bamboo shoots in the boiling water. Refresh, drain and shred. Shred the ham.*

* *Finely chop the ginger and spring onions.*

* *Place the sliced fish on the table. Put the shredded ingredients at one end and roll up, sealing with a little flour.*

* *Sift the flour, baking powder, salt and pepper into a bowl. Add the egg white and water to stir into a smooth batter then blend in both kinds of the oil. Dip the fish rolls into the batter to coat evenly. Heat a wok to bring the oil to boil and deep fry the fish rolls in the hot oil till light brown. Drain and dish. Arrange on the platter between the head and tail.*

* *Heat the wok with the 2 tbsp of oil to sauté the ginger and spring onions. Sizzle the wine and add the sweet sour sauce to bring to the boil. Season to taste. Thicken the sauce with the gravy mix. Drop in the sesame oil to stir well and pour on to the fish rolls. Garnish with the sliced cucumber and serve hot.*

材料：

豬肉1磅（½公斤）　醃料一生抽2湯匙
薑1片　　　　　　糖1湯匙
葱2棵　　　　　　酒½茶匙
蛋1隻　　　　　　胡椒粉少許
菠蘿2片　　　　　生粉1茶匙
青椒1隻　　　　　水3湯匙
紅蘿蔔4安（112克）油2湯匙
沸水3杯
雲耳1湯匙
油4杯　　　　　　調味一鹽¼茶匙
薑絲1茶匙　　　　酒1茶匙
葱頭絲1茶匙　　　酸甜醋½杯

饢料一生粉1茶匙
　　　水1湯匙
　　　蔴油1茶匙

製法：

*　豬肉洗淨抹乾剁碎成肉茸放入碗中
　。薑及葱磨幼與蛋及調味一同放入
　肉茸內和勻撻至起膠，捏成肉丸。
*　菠蘿及青椒皆切粗粒。紅蘿蔔放沸
　水中飛水，取出過冷河隔乾水份亦
　切粗粒。雲耳浸透修剪妥當，放入
　以上沸水中飛水1分鐘。撈起隔乾
　水份候用。
*　燒紅鑊加入油煮沸，放入肉丸以中
　火炸至金黃色，撈起隔去餘油。將
　2湯匙油留在鑊中，其餘盛起別用。
*　再燒熱鑊中油，灑下鹽爆香薑、葱
　絲，隨即加入青椒粒，紅蘿蔔粒及
　雲耳兜勻。濺酒加入酸甜醋再煮沸
　。將肉丸重放入鑊中拌勻，以生粉
　水埋饢，倒入蔴油及菠蘿粒即可上
　碟。

Ingredients:

1 lb (½ kg) pork　4 cups corn oil
1 slice ginger　　1 tsp shredded ginger
2 spring onions　 1 tsp shredded shallot
1 egg
2 pineapple rings
1 capsicum
4 oz (112 g) carrots
3 cups boiling water
1 tbsp black fungus

Marinade-
2 tbsp light soy
1 tbsp sugar
½ tsp wine
a pinch of pepper
1 tbsp cornflour
3 tbsp water
2 tbsp corn oil

Seasoning-
¼ tsp salt
1 tsp wine
½ cup sweet sour sauce

Gravy Mix-
1 tsp cornflour
1 tbsp water
1 tsp sesame oil

Method:

*   Wash, mince and place the pork in
    a mixing bowl. Mince the ginger
    and spring onions finely. Bind the
    pork thoroughly with the chopped
    ginger, spring onions, egg and
    seasoning, then pound until firm.
    Shape into small meatballs.
*   Dice the pineapple and capsicum.
    Blanch the carrots in the boiling
    water. Refresh, drain and dice.
    Soak, trim and blanch the black
    fungus in the same boiling water
    for 1 minute. Rinse and drain.
*   Heat the wok to bring the oil to
    just boil. Deep fry the meatballs
    over moderate heat until golden
    brown. Remove and drain. Pour
    the oil back into the container and
    leave about 2 tbsp in the wok.
*   Reheat the 2 tbsp oil in the wok
    and sprinkle in the salt. Sauté the
    shredded ginger and shallot then
    add the capsicum, carrots and the
    black fungus to stir fry thorough-
    ly. Sizzle the wine and add the
    sweet sour sauce to bring to the
    boil. Return the meatballs into the
    wok to mix well. Thicken the
    sauce with the gravy mix. Stir in
    the sesame oil and pineapple then
    dish and serve.

天降麟兒

Trotters in Sweet Vinegar

材料：

豬手1對每隻約1磅（½公斤）
凍水3杯
蛋6隻
羌3片
另羌2磅（1公斤）

調味－甜醋7杯
　　　米醋1杯
　　　鹽¼茶匙
　　　雞精1粒
　　　糖¼杯

製法：

* 豬手以小刀刮淨，再放火上燒去細毛。洗淨後斬件，再清洗乾淨隔乾水份。
* 煲1隻放入凍水，將蛋洗淨放入烚5分鐘。取出以冷水浸凍，去殼待用。
* 豬手放以上沸水中加羌片煮30分鐘，撈起置水喉下洗淨沖凍隔乾水份。
* 羌浸透後以刀刮淨拍扁，中火乾鑊炒至乾身。
* 瓦煲燒熱，將甜醋倒入煮沸，加入米醋及其他調味料。將羌放入先煮30分鐘，續加豬手煮至酥軟。最後將蛋加入停火浸數小時即可取食。

Ingredients:

1 pair pig's trotters, about 1 lb (½ kg) each
3 cups cold water
6 eggs
3 slices ginger
2 extra lb (1 kg) ginger

Seasoning-
7 cups sweet red vinegar
1 cup rice vinegar
¼ tsp salt
1 cube chicken essence
¼ cup sugar

Method:

* *Scrape and singe the trotters. Clean and chop into pieces. Wash, refresh and drain.*
* *Fill the saucepan with the cold water then put in the eggs to bring to boil. Leave to simmer for 5 minutes. Remove and refresh under a running tap for 5 minutes then shell.*
* *Use the same boiling water to cook the trotters for 30 minutes with the 3 pieces of ginger. Rinse under a running tap and drain.*
* *Soak, scrape and wash the ginger. Pat lightly with the side of a chopper then parch in a hot wok until quite dry.*
* *Heat the earthenware pot and pour in the red vinegar to bring to the boil. Add the rice vinegar and seasoning. Put in the ginger to simmer for 30 minutes. Add the trotters to stew until tender. Turn off the heat and put in the eggs to soak for a few hours before serving.*

Chinese Cookery Terms

1. To **BAKE** is to cook with dry heat, or to dry food with heat.
2. To **BARBEQUE** is to cook meat over a charcoal or wood fire.
3. To **BIND** is to add egg, liquid or melted fat to a mixture in order to hold it together.
4. To **BLANCH** is to immerse the food in boiling water for a short time (from 10 seconds to 5 minutes) in order to tighten the texture, set the colour, or get rid of any unpleasant smell of the food.
5. To **BOIL** is to cook the food in hot bubbling liquid.
6. To **BRAISE** is to finish cooking in a tightly covered wok or saucepan.
7. To **CRIMP** is to slash the surface of a fish at intervals.
8. To **DEEP FRY** is to cook food in a large amount of hot boiling oil in order to make it crispy.
9. To **DOUBLE-BOIL** is to cook in a covered container, which is placed in a covered wok half-filled with boiling water.
10. To **DRAIN** is to remove excess liquid from the ingredients through a strainer or colander.
11. To **DREDGE** is to sprinkle the ingredient with flour or sugar, etc.
12. To **FRY** is to cook with a little hot oil.
13. To **GUT** is to remove the intestine and clean the inside of a fish.
14. To **PARBOIL** is to leave the food in warm oil until half-cooked.
15. To **PARCH** is to brown food in a dry hot wok or frying pan.
16. To **POACH** is to simmer food gently in a liquid which is kept just below boiling point.
17. To **REFRESH** is to rinse the ingredient with cold water after it is blanched. The ingredient is then reheated before serving.
18. To **ROAST** is to prepare the food by using high heat, with flame or over the charcoal.
19. **To SAUTÉ is to stir the ingredients quickly in a wok or pan with a little hot oil, over high heat.**
20. To **SCALD** is to plunge the ingredient into boiling water quickly to make peeling easier or to clean or loosen the hair on the ingredient.
21. To **SHALLOW FRY** is to cook the food in a little oil until both sides are brown.
22. To **SIMMER** is to cook the food or liquid slowly over low heat.
23. To **SMOKE** is to place the food on a rack in a wok or oven filled with smoke.
24. To **STEAM** is to cook the food by putting it into a steamer placed in a wok half-filled with boiling water. Timing begins when the water boils. High heat should be used so that there is enough steam to cook the food quickly.
25. To **STEW** is to cook the food with a little liquid over low heat.
26. To **STIR FRY** is to cook the food quickly in a little oil over medium heat.
27. To **TOSS** is to mix the ingredients evenly by throwing them in a wok and jerking the wok up and down.

The cooking oil used in this book can either be corn oil, vegetable oil, peanut oil or sunflower oil, unless otherwise stated.

烹飪常用術語

焗	—將食物放鑊中蓋密，以文火焗熟。或將拌妥粉料放焗爐中以慢火焗至鬆發。
炭燒	—將食物以叉叉着或放在炭上之鐵網直接以明火燒熟。
搞	—加水或蛋或牛奶在乾材料中和成一糰。
飛水	—將食物放入沸水內稍拖一下，取出洗淨續煮。
焯	—將食物放入沸水中，藉沸水熱力使食物煮熟。與灼及煮略同。灼要手快。
紅燒	—用豉油及水將食物煮熟。與煮及炆略同，有時則與烤之意義相近如燒烤。
炸	—將大量油煮沸，放入食物浸過面，以沸油之熱度使食物炸至酥脆。油炸食品多需上乾粉或濕粉，並要猛油落鑊。
燉	—將食物加配料及水放在燉盅內，再轉放深鍋中加水慢火燉至食品酥爛。食前加調味。此法可保原味，多與補品同燉。
上粉	—將食物以麵粉或糖洒勻在週圍而後按實。
炒	—將鑊燒紅，加少量油煮沸，放入材料迅速兜勻。
泡油	—將食物醃好後，放入猛鑊陰油中泡至油將沸時撈起，隔去油候用。
烙	—以燒熱乾鑊將已洗淨材料文火煮乾後續烙至淺黃色。
浸	—用湯或油煮熟後將火降至將沸未沸之溫度，把食物如鷄或魚等放入，以一定之溫度浸至熟，切不可用猛火。
過冷河	—將食物先用沸水煮過，取出再放冷水中冲凍使其爽脆，麵食多須過冷河。
烤	—以明火將食物炙熟使香氣四溢，用中式烤爐與西式焗爐皆可。
爆	—迅速用猛火將食物以油或醬料加料頭用火逼熟。
灼或燙	—將食物迅速放入沸水中浸片刻然後去皮或拔毛。
煎	—燒紅鑊放少量油將食物僅浸到少許，慢火煎至兩面金黃香脆。
燴	—燒熱鑊鑊，讚酒加上湯，再加已泡油或煮熟之食物及配料煮沸，以粟粉開水少許打饋。
烟或燻	—食物先用調味品醃過，排在已放燻料（糖、蔗片、茶葉等）之鑊中的鐵絲網上。蓋上鑊蓋，藉燻料冒出之烟使食物燻至微黃而有烟味。
蒸	—將食物以碟墊起放蒸籠內蓋密，轉置沸水鑊中以蒸氣使食物致熟。
炆	—先將食物放配料爆炒過，轉放另一密蓋鑊內加水少許，改用文火經長時間炆至食物酥爛汁濃為止。紅炆者熟後加老抽。
拌炒	—此為中國烹飪中最常用之方法，將食物先泡油嫩油至七分熟，然後再燒紅鑊加配料放食物讚酒，迅速兜勻上碟。
抛	—將鑊中食物迅速在大火上抛動，使火力平均。
煮	—將食物放入水中煮，藉沸水之熱力將食品煮至酥爛，然後加調味料。
煲	—將食物放入水中煮滾，改用文火繼續煲至夠火及出味為止。此法通常需時較長。
滷	—用水加滷水料、生抽、紹酒、冰糖等煮至出味。然後把食物飛水後浸在滷水中。浸至入味。滷水盆如處理得宜可長期不變壞。
煨	—將食物放入上湯內慢火煮之，使其吸收上湯味道，或放羌葱水內煨之，以除腥味。
撈拌	—把已煮熟之食物切絲與其他配料放在一起和勻謂之撈。多用於冷盆。
扒	—手法與燴略同，唯汁水較少及較濃。

註：本書食譜內所用之油通常為粟米油，亦可用菜油或花生油。

MEAT MARINADE

Seasoning used / 1 lb (½ kg) of meat	Sugar	Light Soy	Soda Bi-carbonate	Egg White	Cornflour	Wine
🐷	1 tbsp	2 tbsp			1 tbsp	1 tbsp
🐮	1 tbsp	2 tbsp	1½ tsp		1 tbsp	1 tbsp
🐐	1 tbsp	2 tbsp	1 tsp		1 tbsp	1 tbsp
🐔	1 tbsp	1 tbsp		1	1 tbsp	2 tbsp
🦆	1 tbsp	2 tbsp	1 tsp	1	1 tbsp	2 tbsp
🦆	1 tbsp	2 tbsp	2 tsp		1 tbsp	2 tbsp
🕊	1 tsp	1 tbsp		1	1 tbsp	1 tbsp
🐟	1 tbsp	2 tbsp		1	1 tbsp	
🦐				1	2 tbsp	

Ginger Juice	Pepper	Water	Method	Oil	Total Marinate Time
	⅛ tsp	⅓ cup	Mix and leave for 30 minutes	¼ cup	1 hour
	¼ tsp	1 cup	Mix and leave for 1 hour	⅓ cup	2 hours
1 tbsp	¼ tsp	½ cup	Mix and leave for 1 hour	¼ cup	2 hours
2 tbsp	⅛ tsp	⅓ cup	Mix and leave for 10 minutes	⅓ cup	½ hour
2 tbsp	¼ tsp	½ cup	Mix and leave for 1 hour	⅓ cup	2 hours
2 tbsp	¼ tsp	½ cup	Mix and leave for 1 hour	½ cup	2 hours
1 tbsp	⅛ tsp	⅓ cup	Mix and leave for 10 minutes	¼ cup	½ hour
1 tbsp	¼ tsp		Mix		½ hour
	⅛ tsp		Mix		10 minutes

各種肉類醃料份量及時間

1磅 (½公斤) 肉類 ＼ 調味	糖	生抽	鬆肉粉	蛋白	生粉	酒
（猪）	1湯匙	2湯匙			1湯匙	1湯匙
（牛）	1湯匙	2湯匙	1½茶匙		1湯匙	1湯匙
（羊）	1湯匙	2湯匙	1茶匙		1湯匙	1湯匙
（雞）	1湯匙	1湯匙		1	1湯匙	2湯匙
（鵝）	1湯匙	2湯匙	1茶匙	1	1湯匙	2湯匙
（鴨）	1湯匙	2湯匙	2茶匙		1湯匙	2湯匙
（鴿）	1茶匙	1湯匙		1	1湯匙	1湯匙
（魚）	1湯匙	2湯匙		1	1湯匙	
（蝦）				1	2湯匙	

羌汁	胡椒粉	水	方法	油	時間
	$\frac{1}{8}$茶匙	$\frac{1}{3}$杯	拌勻, 置一旁醃30分鐘	$\frac{1}{4}$杯	1 小時
	$\frac{1}{4}$茶匙	1 杯	拌勻, 置一旁醃1 小時	$\frac{1}{3}$杯	2 小時
1 湯匙	$\frac{1}{4}$茶匙	$\frac{1}{2}$杯	拌勻, 置一旁醃1 小時	$\frac{1}{4}$杯	2 小時
2 湯匙	$\frac{1}{8}$茶匙	$\frac{1}{3}$杯	拌勻, 置一旁醃10分鐘	$\frac{1}{3}$杯	$\frac{1}{2}$小時
2 湯匙	$\frac{1}{4}$茶匙	$\frac{1}{2}$杯	拌勻, 置一旁醃1 小時	$\frac{1}{3}$杯	2 小時
2 湯匙	$\frac{1}{4}$茶匙	$\frac{1}{2}$杯	拌勻, 置一旁醃1 小時	$\frac{1}{2}$杯	2 小時
1 湯匙	$\frac{1}{8}$茶匙	$\frac{1}{3}$杯	拌勻, 置一旁醃10分鐘	$\frac{1}{4}$杯	$\frac{1}{2}$小時
1 湯匙	$\frac{1}{4}$茶匙		拌勻		$\frac{1}{2}$小時
	$\frac{1}{8}$茶匙		拌勻		10分鐘

9-Piece Wok Set

A. Turner
B. Ladle
C. 8" copper wire strainer
D. Aluminium wok cover
E. 14" iron wok
F. Steam rack
G. 10" iron wok ring
H. Wok brush
I. Long chopsticks

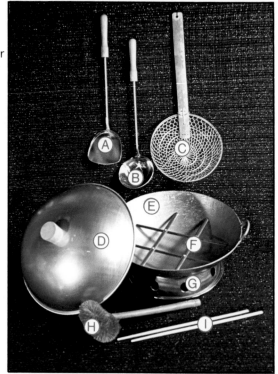

Ricesheet Cooker Set

A.   Ricesheet cooker   B.   Ladle   C.   Muslin

Steamer

A. 6" Steamer set
B. 8" Steamer set
C. 10" Steamer set
D. 12" Steamer set

Hot Pot Set

A. 11" hot pot   B. 10 copper wire scoops   C. 10 pairs chopsticks

Chopsticks Cooking Centre would like to announce that they do not have any branches or affiliates in any cities in South-east Asia, nor have they appointed anyone to run a cookery school in Singapore or elsewhere in Asia. Chopsticks Cooking Centre is managed by Mdm Cecilia J. Au-Yang at 108 Boundary Street, Ground Floor, Kowloon, Hong Kong, and remains the only authentic enterprise registered under this name.

CHOPSTICKS COOKING CENTRE

July 1990

Our Cooking Centre

Chinese Cookery Courses

Chinese Dishes Course
Chinese Roasts Course
Dim Sum Course
Cakes & Pastries Course
Professional Bread-making Course
Bean Curd Course
Moon Cake Course
Piping Course
Wedding Cake Course
Ingredients Course
Banquet Dishes Course
Vegetable Carving Course
Deep Fried Pastry Course

* * * * * * *

½-3 days Tourist Group Course
1 day Selected Course
1-week Tourist Course
4-week Intensive Course
8-week Intensive Course
13-week Professional Course
17-week Teacher Training Course

Length of course:–
    2 hours to 17 weeks

Our Hostel

* Air-conditioning
* Colour T.V.
* Private bath
* Private telephone
* Reasonable rent

3-DAY TOURIST GROUP COURSE

US$300.00 per head for a group of 10 to 15 persons
Schedule as follows–

Time	Day 1	Day 2	Day 3
10 am	2 Chinese dishes	2 Chinese dishes	Market Visit
12 noon	A taste of Chinese dishes	A taste of dim sum	2 dish sum
2 pm	2 dim sum	2 Chinese dishes	2 dim sum
4 pm	Chinese dish practice	Chinese dish practice	Chinese dish practice

嘉饌家政中心暫時尚未在任何國家開設分校。

各式烹飪班

各省中菜班
初高燒烤班
初高點心班
高級西餅班
職業麵包班
馳名豆腐班
速成月餅班
速成唧花班
結婚禮餅班
各式原料班
筵席大菜班
蔬菓雕花班
各式油器班
1/2—3天集體遊客班
1天各科精選班
1週遊客班
4週速成班
8週速成班
13週職業班
17週教師訓練班

專業烹飪導師培訓班
學制分1年，2年及3年
基本移民班
高級移民班

宿舍設備

＊空氣調節
＊彩色電視
＊私家浴室
＊私人電話
＊合理價錢

"CHOPSTICKS RECIPES"

is a symbol of   CONFIDENCE

CHOPSTICKS PUBLICATIONS
a symbol of confidence

The **Chopsticks Recipes** series English-Chinese bilingual edition (128 pp 105 gsm matt art paper) is an encyclopedia to Chinese cuisine, written for people who enjoy trying different kinds of Chinese food in their daily life. Book 1 is an introduction to a variety of cooking while each of the other 11 books contain one specific subject.

Book 1 — **introduction**
Book 2 — **Dim Sum**
Book 3 — **Traditional Dishes**
Book 4 — **Quick Meals**
Book 5 — **Everyday Menus**
Book 6 — **Cakes and Bread**
Book 7 — **Vegetarian Dishes**
Book 8 — **More Dim Sum**
Book 9 — **Budget Meals**
Book 10 — **Chinese Casseroles**
Book 11 — **Healthy Bean Dishes**
Book 12 — **Vegetable Carvings**

First Steps in Chinese Cooking and **More Steps in Chinese Cooking** English-Chinese bilingual edition (96 pp 115 gsm matt art paper) each contains 42 specially written recipes which have been tested by children from the ages of 8 to 14 years. These book are designed for parents and children to learn Chinese cooking together.

Other Chopsticks publications include **Chopsticks Cookery Cards** Grades 1 and 2 English-Chinese bilingual edition (260 gsm B/S coated art board with pp lamination)

Chopsticks Recipes revised English Edition (128 pp 128 gsm matt art paper)

Chopsticks Wok Miracles English-Chinese bilingual edition (128 pp 128 gsm matt art paper)

Utensils Order Form

Please quote me the prices for the following items:-

A. _____ 9-piece Wok Set _ _ _ _ _ _ _ _ _ _ _ US$ _____
B. _____ Chinese Casserole _ _ _ _ _ _ _ _ _ _ US$ _____
C. _____ Hot Pot Set _ _ _ _ _ _ _ _ _ _ _ _ US$ _____
D. _____ Ricesheet Cooker _ _ _ _ _ _ _ _ _ _ US$ _____
E. Baking Utensils

_____ US$ _____
_____ US$ _____

F. Bamboo Steamer Set with 2 Tiers & 1 Lid
_____ 8″ Steamer Set _ _ _ _ _ _ _ _ _ _ _ US$ _____
_____ 12″ Steamer Set _ _ _ _ _ _ _ _ _ _ US$ _____

G. Cutters
_____ Fish _____ Bird _____ Butterfly US$ _____
_____ Cock _____ Rabbit _____ Pig US$ _____

H. Dim Sum Utensils

_____ US$ _____
_____ US$ _____

I. Dry Ingredients for Mail Order
_____ kg Black Mushrooms _ _ _ _ _ _ _ _ US$ _____
_____ kg Dried Shrimps _ _ _ _ _ _ _ _ _ US$ _____
_____ kg Spicy Salt _ _ _ _ _ _ _ _ _ _ _ US$ _____
_____ kg Dried Scallops _ _ _ _ _ _ _ _ _ US$ _____
_____ kg Shrimp Roe _ _ _ _ _ _ _ _ _ _ US$ _____
_____ kg Agar Agar _ _ _ _ _ _ _ _ _ _ _ US$ _____

J. Wooden Cake Moulds

_____ US$ _____
_____ US$ _____

Registered p & p (Airmail) _ _ _ _ _ _ _ _ _ _ _ _ _ _ _ _ _
US$ _____

_____ (Surface Mail) _ _ _ _ _ _ _ _ _ _ _ _ _ _ _
US$ _____

Total Cost US$ _____

Note — Surface mail takes about 60 days for delivery while airmail needs
about 10 days.